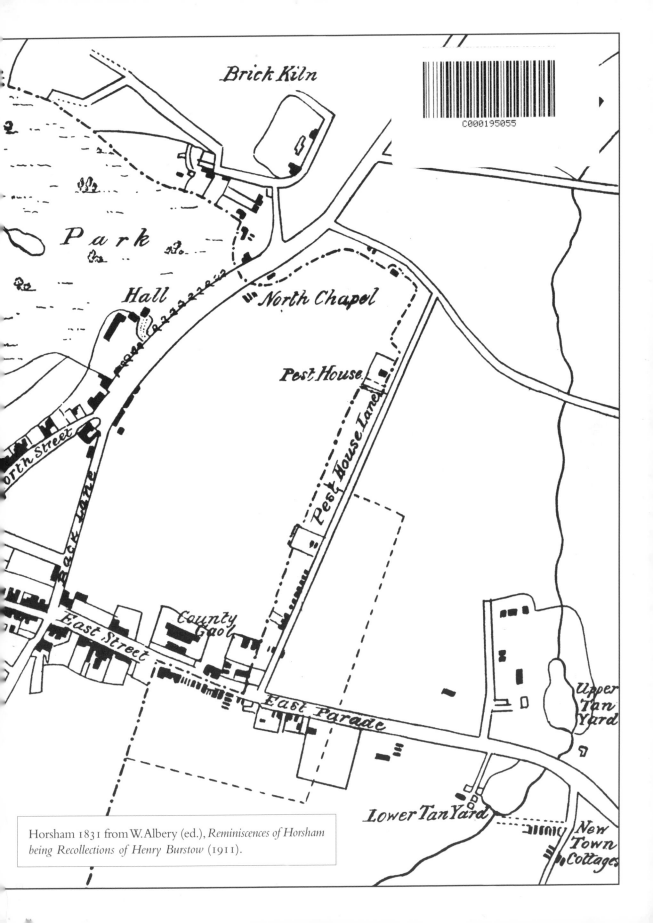

Brick Kiln

Park

Hall

North Chapel

North Street

Pest House

Back Lane

Pest House Lane

County Gaol

East Street

East Parade

Upper Tan Yard

Lower Tan Yard

New Town Cottages

C000195055

Horsham 1831 from W. Albery (ed.), *Reminiscences of Horsham being Recollections of Henry Burstow* (1911).

To Maureen

Happy reading!.

Best wishes from
Sue

29th September 2005.

HORSHAM

A History

The almshouses in the Normandy are in the left foreground with the Priest's House close to the parish church. Poorhouses have been on this site since 1477. The name 'Normandy' may have an association with the Norman de Braose family. There was a well here, supposed to have been used by the Brotherhood. Churchwarden Accounts record in 1645 'the Normandy Well repaired with timber posts', but no trace remains of it today.

HORSHAM

A History

Susan Haines

Phillimore

2005

Published by
PHILLIMORE & CO. LTD,
Shopwyke Manor Barn, Chichester, West Sussex, England

© Susan Haines, 2005

ISBN 1 86077 332 X

Printed and bound in Great Britain by
CAMBRIDGE PRINTING

To my husband
Geoffrey Haines

Contents

List of Illustrations

Frontispiece: Old Almshouses and Priest's House in the Normandy, 1821

Acknowledgements

I am most grateful to Sue Djabri, Dr Annabelle Hughes, Jeremy Knight, Curator of Horsham Museum, and Sylvia Standing for their help, constructive criticism and encouragement. Also the staff at the following places: Chichester, Horsham, Midhurst and Worthing Libraries, Christ's Hospital School, East Sussex Record Office (hereafter ESRO), Horsham District Council (hereafter HDC), Horsham Museum and the Horsham Museum Society, Leeds Museums and Galleries, Royal & SunAlliance, Surrey History Centre, the British Library, the Library at Friends House, London, the Royal Pavilion, Libraries & Museums Brighton, *West Sussex County Times* (hereafter WSCT), West Sussex County Council (hereafter WSCC), West Sussex County Council Sites and Monuments Record, West Sussex Record Office (hereafter WSRO).

I am grateful to the following organisations and institutions for permission to reproduce these illustrations: the British Library, 11 (Maps C.7 c.5 (43)), 37 (Add. 5673 frame 1), 44 (B.8 or C.7.c.1), 60 (Maps 52.d.5), 68 (Add.5675 f10), 72 (Add.5673 f12), 74 (Add.5673 f12), 79 (Add.5673 f13); Christ's Hospital, Horsham, 118-20, 123, 124; Horsham Museum, 5, 14 (Ms No.237), 22, 45, 49, 65 (Ms No.200.6), 67 (Ms No.2801), 69 (Ms No.2802), 81, 82; the Horsham Press, 107; the Horsham Society, 56, 102, 108; © JB Associated Newspapers Ltd, 145; Leeds Museum and Galleries (Temple Newsam House), 61, 62, 63, 66; Middleton Press Collection, 97, 98, 140, 143; Phillimore & Co. Ltd, 76; Stonyhurst College, 35; Weald and Downland Museum, Singleton, 21; West Sussex County Library Service, www.westsussexpast.org.uk/pictures, 6, 15, 83, 88 (P1026), 95, 116 (P1045); © WSCT, 144; WSRO, 6 (PH14546), 10 (PH1101), 28 (PH2058), 37 (Sussex Archaeological Society, Sussex Archaeological Collections Vol.5), 38 (PAR 106/9/1 f1), 46 (PH13048), 47 (Neg.5681), 55 (PD2279), 68 (Sussex Views f81, Sussex Record Society), 71 (Add.Ms 6673), 72 (Sussex Depicted, Sussex Record Society Vol.85), 73 (Add.Ms 1834), 74 (Sussex Views f82, Sussex Record Society), 77 (E102/K/19/89), 78 (Add. Ms 14861), 79 (Sussex Depicted, Sussex Record Society Vol.85), 84 (Add.Ms 1432), 86 (MP1551), 87 (QDD/6/W8), 94, 99 (Add.Ms 19135), 101 (PH8179), 104 (Add.Ms 19135), 106 (PH741), 111 (PAR/106/4/4), 129 (MP1509), 150 (PD1655), 153 (PD1486), and rear endpaper (PM 132-7).

I would like to thank all those individuals who have been so generous in sharing their memories with me, lending me photographs and other material for this book, and granting permission for reproduction of the following illustrations: Renira Barclay, 36; Jane Bowen, 9, 85, 89, 90, 128, 135, 137, 145; John Bray, 56, 102, 108; Eric Bright, 3; Charles Burrell, 47; George Carsten, 159; John & Pauline Cox, 13; Cecil Cramp, 20, 103, 110, 134; Dr John Dew, 115, 125, 144; Sue Djabri, 64; Sabrina Harcourt-Smith, 8, 27; Alicia Hemming, 39, 53, 100, 138; Richard and Shirley Hewitson, 159; Roy Holder, 143; the Revd Antony Hurst, 64; the late Dorothy Leslie, 107; Lord Lytton, 73; David McDowell, 130-3; Maurvian Oakey, 30, 34, 40, 41, 43, 48, 51, 52, 54, 80, 92, 112, 113, 114, 117, 121, 122, 139, 142, 146, 147, 149, 152; Wendy Page, 7; Maggie Parsons, 31; Dr Nowell Peach, 109; John Scrace, 97, 98, 140; Brian Slyfield, 35, 58, 75, 96, 126, 127, 148; Anthony Sparrow, 82; Canon Derek Tansill, frontispiece, 4, 16, 24, 29, 32; the Rt Revd Lindsay Urwin, 36; Graham Wakefield, 50, 91, 93, 105, 141, 156; Tony Wales, 19. Thanks also to Geoffrey Haines for taking the following photographs: 1, 17, 18, 21, 57, 81, 136, 154, 155, 158; and to Norman Perry for photographing the pictures for the dustjacket and frontispiece. Illustrations 23, 25, 33 and 70 are taken from D.E. Hurst's *History and Antiquities of Horsham* (1889).

Every effort has been made to reach the copyright holders of illustrations nos 9, 39, 100, 125, 128, 135, 137, 142 and 145. I would be glad to hear from anyone whose rights have been infringed unknowingly so that an acknowledgement is given in any future edition.

I am also indebted to these people who have assisted me in various ways: Roy Bayliss, Richard Chasemore, Oriel Cocksworth, Christine Costin, Molly Cramp, Pauleen Crowder, Lucy Forster, John Fowler, Richard Grinham, Frank King, Roger Lintott, Andrew Marshall, Vic Mitchell, Stuart Neal, Charles Page, Cyril Sargent, Guy Scoular, Joan Stanley, Shirley Steers, William Tyrrell, John Veitch, Brad Watson and Eileen Wield. So many people have been kind enough to help me and I do apologise if I have inadvertently omitted anyone's name.

ONE

Reaching Back into the Ancient Past

On a clear day a magnificent panoramic view of the Sussex Weald can be obtained from a viewpoint such as Box Hill, Surrey, astride the North Downs Way. The forested ridges and vales and the outline of the blue-grey South Downs 25 miles to the south can be seen clearly. This region, lying between the chalk hills of the North and South Downs, was once covered in forest. The Romans called it *Silva Anderida* and the Saxons named it *Andredsweald*. From the vantage point on the North Downs it can be seen that woodland still predominates, despite human interference, and West Sussex remains one of the most heavily wooded counties in England.

1   *This view of the Sussex Weald is taken from Salomons Memorial, Box Hill, Surrey looking south towards the English Channel. Although Horsham is not visible, the railway line from Dorking to Horsham can be seen cutting through the trees in the far distance, halfway between the left and centre of the picture.*

	Sandstones and Wadhurst clay
	Clay
	Lower Greensand
	Upper Greensand and Gault
	Chalk
	Clays, sands and gravels

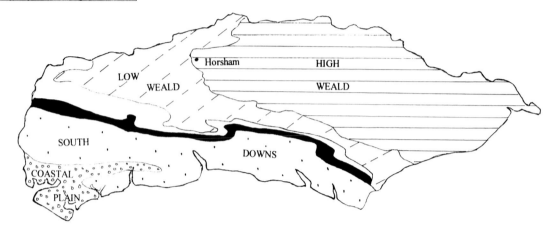

2 *Geology of the region showing Horsham at the north-western edge of the sandstone High Weald.*

3 *This drawing is by the late Sylvia Bright. The earliest part of the building, towards the rear, is medieval, but there have been later additions. During the 16th century this was probably the home of a wealthy merchant. It was first used as a museum c.1940-1. The Horsham Museum and Tourist Information Centre now occupy the building.*

The region has not always looked like this and there have been immense changes in the geology, climate and morphology of the landscape. From *c.*140 million years ago, during the geological period known as the Cretaceous, the Wealden beds of Horsham were deposited in a vast flood plain that stretched from London to Paris, westwards to Dorset and eastwards to Belgium. Huge rivers flowed into the flood plain – one from the Cornish area and another from the north, and these deposited iron-rich silts, which were to provide much of the ore for the Wealden iron industry, and alternating clays, sand and limestone in ever-moving channels.

The climate then was warm and there may have been marked wet and dry periods. The rich plant, fish and insect life attracted dinosaurs, including iguanodons. George Bax Holmes, an avid collector of fossils and dinosaur bones, who was born in Horsham in 1803 and lived for a time in the Causeway, made a most exciting discovery in the 19th century. The femur and other bones of an iguanodon were discovered when workmen were digging the foundations of the Chapel of Ease, which became St Mark's Church, in the centre of Horsham in 1840. Known as 'The Great Horsham Iguanodon', the fossil remains were used as the basis for the model iguanodon created by the sculptor Benjamin Waterhouse Hawkins, who was commissioned to construct full-size replicas of the known dinosaurs at the time. These were installed in the Crystal Palace grounds, Sydenham, South London, following the Great Exhibition of 1851. Holmes came into contact with Richard Owen, the first superintendent of the British Museum and the man who coined the term *dinosauria,* and Gideon Mantell, the Sussex surgeon and geologist, who found and described the first iguanodon.

Other bones of iguanodons have been uncovered, at Southwater Brickworks, Clockhouse Brickworks in Capel and Ockley Brickworks. Further interesting finds were made in the 1980s at Rudgwick Brickworks, including fossilised ferns, dragonflies and crocodile bones. In 1985 Mrs Sylvia Standing excavated the fossilised remains of a dinosaur identified as a polacanthus. This particular specimen appears to be unique and has become known as the *Polacanthus Rudgwickensis.* Mrs Standing had previously found many artefacts dating from later prehistoric periods during field-walking in the parishes of Southwater and Nuthurst in the 1960s and 1970s. Many of these prehistoric finds are exhibited at the Horsham Museum.

About 110 million years ago the land slowly subsided and the sea advanced into the flood plain. Marine deposits were laid down, ending with calcareous deposits that later consolidated into chalk. Subsequent earth movements folded the land into a huge upfold, flanked by subsidiary upfolds. The rocks that covered Horsham were eroded away by newly formed rivers to reveal the older sandstones and clays beneath.

The earliest inhabitants in Sussex belong to the Lower and Middle Palaeolithic (Old Stone Age) periods. At this time Britain was a wild frontier on the edge of a continent that stretched from Spain to Japan. Human hunting groups gathered food and set up small camps to catch migrating game. These humans made stone tools, mostly hand axes, from lumps of flint. In Sussex plentiful deposits of flint were to be found in riverbeds, on the Downs and on the shoreline, which has altered many

4 *St Mark's Church before demolition left only the spire.*

times and was not then where it is today. It is
the discovery of these axes that indicates the
presence of humans.

Flint hand axes have been found near
Horsham in the Pulborough area, Steyning,
Rudgwick and St Leonard's Forest. Some of
these are about 200,000 years old. A quartzite
hand axe was found at Southwater. Further
evidence that the earliest humans inhabited
this area comes from a site at Nutbourne, near
Pulborough, where an assemblage of some 2,300
struck flints was found when a drive was cut
through a slope in the 19th century. The site
appears to have been a rock shelter overlooking
a valley and can be put into a date range of
c.28000-14000 B.C.

About 10,000 years ago the last of the ice
sheets finally melted. Britain emerged with a
covering of pine and birch forests. Hunter-
gatherers moved across Britain, following
migrating game in the wildwoods. Areas of
woodland were chopped down by humans using
flint axes, which during this period were hafted,
with an antler sleeve acting as a shock absorber.
As the climate warmed the woodlands changed

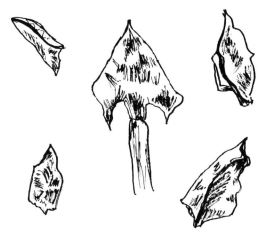

5 *These artefacts are on display at the Horsham
Museum. In the centre is a Bronze-Age arrowhead,
2cm high. Surrounding it are the microliths known
as 'Horsham Points'. They vary between 1.5-2.5cm
in height.*

to a rich deciduous forest of oak, ash and elder.
It was during this Mesolithic (Middle Stone
Age) period that rising sea levels, caused by
melting ice, eventually cut Britain off from the
continent of Europe.

About 6000 B.C. there was a great expansion
in the number of sites in the western Weald. The
Horsham area was extensively settled during the
Mesolithic period and significant discoveries
have been made, including those at Halt, Old
Beeding Wood and Colgate. New styles of flint
work appear on these sites and Horsham has
become world famous in archaeology for its
Mesolithic material. Very small flint implements
called microliths found in the Horsham area are
characterised by numbers of obliquely pointed
and basally retouched points. They are known
as 'Horsham Points'. Excavations at Halt, to the
north-east of Horsham close to the A264, have
recorded a Mesolithic flint assemblage, which
included 649 classified microliths and 1,152
unclassified and fragmentary microliths amongst
other scraping, cutting tools and micro-cores.
It is most likely that the microliths were made
from flint deposits in the South Downs. Hunting
and foraging parties may have brought them
into the area or there may have been trade
links between sites in the Horsham area and
on the Downs.

The microliths, with their razor-sharp edges,
made effective tools. It is thought, and archaeological evidence supports this, that they were
bedded into wood or bone to create composite
tools, such as scrapers, or barbed harpoons for
fishing. Scrapers had several uses, which included
the removal of fur from animal skins after the
skins had been soaked in stale urine, and the
preparation of vegetable products.

There have been many other finds on
isolated sites and scatters, especially to the
south and east of Horsham. These include
hammer-stones and cores. The former were
used to strike flint flakes from a nodule or
core, which had one surface made flat to form

6 *A view of Horsham from Denne Park, which was created in the 17th century, cutting off the main routeway south out of the town. The land was left undeveloped, and residents in the town were able to enjoy it for recreation. Here the parish church dominates the view.*

a striking platform. The thin flat asymmetrical flakes were then worked by hand using either a piece of antler or bone or a flint fabricator. In the 1920s there was a discovery of these at Denne Park. South-west of Horsham, at Pilfolds Farm, struck flakes from a working floor were discovered when the A24 Horsham bypass, which runs close to the rear of the farm, was under construction from 1975-7. Tranchet axes have been found, such as the one unearthed in a ploughed field at Roffey Hurst. This type of axe had a sharp cutting edge, which was produced by removing flakes at right angles to the main axis. Further examples of Mesolithic activity in the vicinity include the discovery of awls (pointed tools used for piercing leather) and burins (chisel-like implements used for engraving bone or antlers).

There are signs that use was made of natural rock-shelters, perhaps when out in hunting parties, particularly in the High Weald. Excavations at Hermitage Rocks, High Hurstwood and High Rocks, Tunbridge Wells have revealed significant Mesolithic finds together with a hearth constructed of sandstone blocks at the Hermitage Rocks.

The arrival of Neolithic activity began in Sussex *c.*4300 B.C. Signs of a more settled lifestyle are apparent with pottery making and the domestication of animals, which was mixed in with hunting, fishing and food gathering. The development of a stone axe trade is also a feature of the period, with axes from Langdale in the Lake District being found across the county.

The building of long barrows, causewayed enclosures and flint mines occurs on the South

Downs. There have been very few Neolithic finds around Horsham, in contrast to the Mesolithic period, although a new type of axe, the polished axe, has been discovered on two sites to the south-east of the town. A Ministry Farm Inspector discovered one in a ploughed field at Whytings Farm in c.1963 whilst the other, at Hornbrook Nurseries, was uncovered some six years later when roses were being planted. Another polished axe has been found near Hills Place. Axes were polished because the shockwaves as the axe hit the wood went around the surface of the axe, rather than causing the flint to shatter. Other local finds – arrowheads, some daggers, a mace head, knife, saw, chisel and scrapers – indicate that a range of tools was used.

The introduction of metals was a marked step forward in the development of technology. Small items of metal were made during the Copper Age, which preceded the Bronze Age – the period in which man started to make bronze metalwork by mixing copper and tin, that began c.2200 B.C. in Britain. The skill may have been introduced by the 'Beaker Folk', who came from the Low Countries and are so called after the distinctive shape of their pottery drinking vessels. Alternatively it may have been brought in through trade or through the spread of knowledge by individuals. Initially bronze was used to make ornaments and other personal possessions, displaying the owner's status in society, but as it became more widely available it was used to make household goods and tools.

The distribution of bronze flat axes in the Weald demonstrates that this area came to be exploited on a large scale, and tracts of forest cover were removed, gradually changing to heathland. Tools found locally include an early Bronze-Age axe at Colgate and the fragment of a socketed axe on the site of Christ's Hospital. Barbed and tanged arrowheads, signifying that hunting weapons were becoming more powerful and effective, with arrowheads able to pierce the skins of animals, have been found to the south of

Horsham. Another remarkably preserved artefact is a skull, which was unearthed in 1933 in Cricket Field Road.

The discovery of a Faience bead at Parkes Farm, to the south of Southwater, is indicative of trading, as is a broken bronze axe found to the north-east of Horsham at Shepherdsfield, which is of Irish origin.

The practice of building round burial chambers, or round barrows, where an individual was inhumed in a crouching position or cremated, was a feature of the Early Bronze Age. One such burial site called 'Money Mound', about four and a half miles from Horsham on the sandstone ridge in Lower Beeding parish, north of Hammerpond Road near Ashfold Crossways, has been excavated. No burial has been found owing to the acidity of the soil, but finds include a beaker, knives, rivets and a fine barbed and tanged arrowhead. Evidence that this site had been occupied at an earlier date is provided by the excavation of Mesolithic flint pieces, five microliths and some smooth pebbles that would have been used as sling stones or as fishing weights, for naturally occurring objects were used as tools. The site attracted attention during the later Iron Age as pottery and beads dating from that period have also been found. Interest continued later, as Roman and Romano-British pottery and 156 coins appear to have been deliberately buried there, perhaps for votive offerings. No traces remain of this site today.

As native people learnt to use iron, bronze was replaced as an implement and weapon. During the Iron Age society was structured and well-organised, with strong military overtones. European invaders took over large areas and so there was a rise in the number of hillforts and arms. In Sussex most settlements were in the south, on the Downs and near the coast, but during the first century B.C. (the Late Iron Age) iron workings were established in the Weald. The area contained an abundance of the basic materials that were needed, with its iron ore deposits in the wealden clay, sandstones, which were used in furnace making, and plentiful supplies of timber, especially oak, which could be used for fuel and building. There were Iron-Age settlements at Goffs Park and Southgate West, Crawley, where smelting of gold and copper was also in operation. Excavations have established iron making at Broadfield from the first century B.C.

Some artefacts have been discovered locally. A glimpse into the domestic side of life is provided by a loom weight that was found at Chesworth Farm and would have been used in weaving cloth, an activity that was developed widely during this time. A fragment of East Sussex Ware pottery that is Late Iron Age/Roman has been dug up at Chennells Brook Farm. A Romano-British blue glass bead, which is a rare find and may indicate an association with an Iron-Age tribe, has been found on Jackrells Farm to the east of Southwater.

Julius Caesar and his troops visited Britain in 55 B.C. but the Romans did not come to settle until A.D. 43. The impact of their invasion in Sussex was significant, with the construction of some major roads, built initially for military purposes. Stane Street connected London (*Londinium*) with Chichester (*Noviomagus*), a town created by the Roman imperial government, and the rapidly growing and important developments around Chichester Harbour and Fishbourne Palace. The A29 from Pulborough through Billingshurst to Alfoldean roundabout shadows the Roman road. Stane Street was used as a north-south transportation route, becoming in the process an important commercial highway during the period of Roman occupation. Latter-day Horsham was relatively close to this highway and two associated posting stations, or *mansiones*, at Hardham (near Pulborough) and Alfoldean, which is less than four miles away. The *mansiones* were part of the imperial communications system and provided accommodation for official travellers, and possibly also some local policing and administrative functions.

7 *Watercolour on vellum by Wendy Page, botanical illustrator, depicting apples growing in her Horsham garden. The painting is in the archive of the Hunt Institute for Botanical Documentation at the Carnegie Mellon University, Pittsburgh, USA. Her work is also held at the Chelsea Physic Garden archive. She has exhibited widely and received numerous commissions in England and abroad, including two works for the Horsham Museum.*

The most important industry in Roman Sussex was iron making, particularly as the Romans needed iron to supply the troops. This meant that the iron-rich Weald was quickly exploited, especially during the second century. There were two main groups of ironworks: an eastern area linked to the Roman navy, the *Classis Britannica,* and a western zone which lay to the east of Horsham. The Iron-Age settlements in the Crawley area were taken over by the Romans for iron working. Broadfield was an important centre with at least 36 furnaces; a Romano-British bloomery continued into the fourth century until Roman social and economic life declined in Sussex. Much closer to Horsham was a tile workings at Baystone, about one mile south-west of the town, which provided tiles for the *mansio* at Alfoldean. There were also potteries in the Hardham-Pulborough-Wiggonholt area in the Arun Valley vicinity. Stane Street and a second Roman road called the Greensand Way,

8 *Hills Place by William Penstone from* A History of the Castles, Mansions and Manors of Western Sussex *by Elwes & Robinson, 1876. The Hills Place estate was broken up after 1819 and the Middleton house pulled down, leaving only the Elizabethan farmhouse, which was demolished in c.1925, and the Georgian additions, which remained until the 1980s.*

which was the route from Pulborough running east along the foot of the Downs, would have been used for transportation.

In view of the Roman activity in the surrounding area, it is perhaps surprising that so little from this period has been found in the Horsham vicinity. One possible reason for this is that Roman evidence has not been discovered because it is hidden underneath existing buildings and roads. In 1962 a quernstone (a stone hand mill for grinding corn) was discovered when the General Post Office was erecting a telephone junction box just outside the Hills Place site on Guildford Road opposite Merryfield Drive. In 1986 the Museum Society archaeology sub-group made a significant discovery of Roman pottery on nearby Hills Place land, which was being excavated prior to development. About 400 pieces of pottery dating from the second century A.D. were found in what may have been a rubbish pit. The pieces seemed to be mainly coarse kitchen pottery. The people who used this pottery may have been Roman or British. The pit may have been near to a rural settlement, perhaps a farm or villa or even a mill, but no remains have been discovered.

Other finds, whilst not necessarily indicating actual settlement in the vicinity, include coins from Denne Road, such as one of Emperor Septimus Severus (A.D. 193-211) which a workman spotted. Denne Road was a prehistoric and Romano-British trackway and a first-century A.D. Romano-British pot rim has been discovered in Southwater Street which continues the line of track. Some fibulae in a grave, together with two first-century brooches, have been found to the south of the town. There may well be other treasures as yet undiscovered.

TWO

The Dawning of a New Town

Many of the inhabitants who lived in the south of the county drove their animals north every year to feed on the woodland pastures of the High Weald. Denne Hill to the south of Horsham was one of the earliest places to be used for grazing by herdsmen coming up from Washington manor about twelve miles to the south ('Denne' was very specifically a 'swine pasture'). Over time some people decided to stay permanently, taking advantage of the water supply, farming land and timber – all essential factors for settlement.

Horsham was on one of these northward tracks on the western edge of the High Weald at a point where the river Arun could be forded. It became a spot favoured by horse breeders and traders, as its name indicates. The animals were grazed in the wet winter months on the relatively drier ground of the sandstone countryside in St Leonard's Forest, away from the boggy mud near the river. Horsham is first mentioned in an Anglo-Saxon land charter of A.D. 947 as an outlier of the manor of Washington – outliers were detached and often scattered

9 A bedecked shire horse. Horsham is believed to have got its name from 'Horse-ham', which means 'place of horses'. In the past people thought the name of Horsham was associated with Horsa and Hengist, the semi-legendary fifth-century Jute mercenaries, but this view is now discredited. Hengist Close alludes to this legend.

10 *Denne Road, described in 17th-century church terriers (descriptions of glebe lands, tithes and dues payable to the vicar) as 'a great highway from Southwater to the heath'. The road has also been called Back Lane and Friday Lane.*

holdings belonging to a manor. *Ceoldred's worth* (Chesworth) and *rogh hay* (Roffey), meaning dear enclosure, are also surviving place-names from that era, with the implications of isolated farmstead and hunting grounds.

The original site has never been discovered. It was probably around the junction of East Street and Denne Road – the ancient north-south route that crossed the river Arun and went over Denne Hill. The Saxons built in timber but, as this is not as durable as stone, wooden buildings have disappeared, or possibly remain undiscovered below later construction. A vivid stretch of the imagination is needed to compare the vast spread of the town today with the simple settlement of the Saxons.

Following William of Normandy's conquest in 1066 Sussex was divided up into five (later six) units called rapes running north from the coast. These were based on an existing administrative framework of hundreds. The county was strategically important for it played a vital part in communications between London and Normandy. Each rape had a port and a castle with secondary fortifications in a chain stretching northwards. Ownership of land passed from Saxon into Norman hands as William the Conqueror gave rapes to his trusted barons. Bramber rape was given to William de Braose. His castle was at Bramber. Today this is just a ruin in a small village but then it commanded the river Adur. The port was at Shoreham. Horsham was near the fortified sites of Chennelsbrook, Sedgwick and Knepp. These were all within a seven-mile radius of Horsham. This meant that a day's return journey for trade could be made between the fortifications and Horsham.

11 *The Bramber rape as depicted on Speed's map (after John Norden's map of 1595). It is full of fascinating, minute detail and is highly decorative, although no roads are shown. Horsham is depicted as a market town and Chesworth as a 'House of a Gentleman'.*

In December 1085 William the Conqueror commissioned a great survey to assess the amount of land and resources owned in England at the time and the extent of the taxes he could raise. Despite the detail recorded in Domesday Book in 1086 the settlement of Horsham is not mentioned. This may have been because it was not of any financial value and so was not written down. The A.D. 947 charter shows that it existed although it is not known if it was a nucleated or dispersed settlement. Horsham is probably included in the entry for Washington. Yet within the space of 200 years it had become a town with borough status and had gained the privilege of sending two representatives to Parliament. It has been possible to identify Marlpost as four hides held by William de Braose from the Archbishop of Canterbury. This lay to the west of the later borough, eventually extending from Marlpost Farm in Southwater up to Porter's Farm in Rusper.

12 *The de Braose crest has a lion rampant and a field covered with small crosslets. The borough arms were derived from those of de Braose. The lordship of the manor passed through marriage to the Dukes of Norfolk. Taken from Horsfield's* History of Sussex.

The de Braose base at Chesworth may have been used first as a hunting lodge for chasing the deer in St Leonard's Forest, that 'vast unfrequented place, full of unwholesome shades and shadows'. Chesworth was among the meadows and is about half a mile south-east of the parish church. It became the manor house for Horsham, and a park was in existence by 1271. The de Braoses had the honour, and expense, of entertaining Edward I and Edward II in 1299 and 1324 respectively. It was partly due to the patronage of this family, who spotted the potential of Horsham, that the settlement developed into a significant trading and commercial centre at the northern end of the Bramber rape.

Sometime in the first decade of the 1200s de Braose, as lord of the manor, separated out an area of land within the manor and turned it into a borough. Records refer to Horsham as a borough in 1235 and 1248. The boundaries of it included what are now North, South, East and West Streets and the Carfax. He designated 52 distinct plots or burgages around a newly formed marketplace. These were irregular in shape and some were curiously sited, suggesting that they were formed out of existing land plots. They had a status in law that meant they had to remain the same. They were passed down in families and could be owned by women. The plots did change hands, for they could be bought and sold, and possession of a burgage plot was keenly sought. The medieval pattern of settlement in Horsham created by the formation of the borough has been retained, influencing the present-day layout of the town centre.

An example of an original burgage house is the property known as 'Bishops'. This imposing medieval timber-framed house is at the junction of East Street and Denne Road and now houses the Pizza Piazza.

The owners of the burgages were known as burgesses. They swore fealty, or loyalty, to de Braose but escaped manorial service by paying a shilling a year instead. The burgesses,

13 *East Street viewed from the east end in the early part of the last century. The street may have grown out of an alleyway that joined Denne Road with today's South Street and marketplace. Evidence relating to a property called 'Vigoures Mead' has enabled identification of buildings in East Street with the site of a range of shops built c.1340.*

14 *This burgage tenement is on the east side of the Carfax. Today it contains offices and a shop. Originally it was a single house built on the site known as the Chequer.*

15 *'Oyez! Oyez! Oyez!' Known to children as 'Billy La La', a jubilant William Law, the last Town Crier in Horsham, has just won the first national championship for Town Criers held in Devizes, Wiltshire in 1912. After his success he was chaired around the Carfax accompanied by combined town bands.*

who carried a considerable degree of authority, became the leading townsmen and ran the affairs of the borough, controlling the administration and laws. For instance, they decided on the rents that traders had to pay for their stalls on market days and established the regulations for the training of apprentices, and for hiring and dismissing workmen. They held their own court, known as the Court Leet, and appointed local officials annually – such as the bailiffs who ran administrative affairs, the headboroughs and constables, who looked after law and order, the aleconners and leather searchers and the Town Crier, which was a permanent appointment. Every male who lived in the borough area for a year and a day came under its jurisdiction. Various people were 'presented' for offences such as failing to keep the highway outside their homes free of rubbish or for not clearing ditches and privies. Those who cheated on their customers, and sold short weight or adulterated goods, were punished.

Total independence was not quite gained, however, since the court was presided over by the lord's steward, who was therefore a powerful man. The de Braose family continued to exert their right and duty to hold a manorial Court Baron within the borough at intervals. Either the lord or his steward presided over this court, which dealt with matters relating to administration, rights and privileges, admitting tenants, registering deaths of burgesses and transferring burgages. Another borough court was the Portmoot Court or Three Weeks Court, and this dealt with trespass and debt cases under 40 shillings.

Horsham was created for trade, and its importance grew with the granting of charters. It was also in the interest of de Braose to develop trade because he kept a percentage of the profits and tolls. In 1233 a Royal Charter of Henry III granted William de Braose a market and an annual Fair that could last up to nine days. The fair took place in July at the Feast of St Thomas. Later de Braose claimed the right to hold two markets, on Saturdays and Wednesdays, making the most of Horsham's position as a natural communication centre on the north-west corner of the High Weald. The marketplace would have covered the whole area from the top of the Causeway to the north end of Carfax.

The market stalls tended to be grouped together in a random fashion with dealers in similar trades or produce collecting together to

16 *The Carfax is first named in 1524/5 as 'The Skarfolkes' and in 1548 as the 'street called Scarfax'. The name may have derived from the fact that the place was a large empty expanse, unpopulated or 'scarce of folks'. In the late 18th century spelling was standardised and the Scarfax was renamed the Carfax.*

17 *The building on the left used to be the* Green Dragon Inn *and the one on the right the* Talbot *or* Wonder Inn. *Both were burgage properties that were, in time, divided into several parts to increase the votes.*

ply their wares. Thus the place where the cattle were slaughtered was in Butcher's Row. In time permanent buildings replaced the temporary structures, forming 'islands' which exist today in the modern town centre. None of the dwellings on these 'islands' was on a burgage plot so the owners of the properties had no say in the running of the town. The narrow passageways in between the stalls have been preserved in Colletts Alley, Glynde Place and Middle Street, which was formerly Butcher's Row. Other alleyways

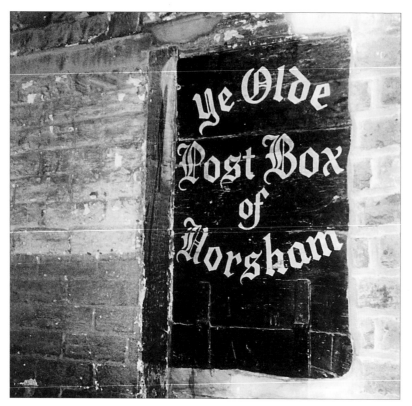

18 This building was the first post office in Horsham. The 'window' letter box dates from 1830 and consists of a wooden hinged panel in the entrance to Pump Alley.

19 Market day in the Bishopric. The road was wide enough for cattle pens to be erected on both sides of the street. These pens featured on the 1897 6-inch Ordnance Survey map of the town. The market was forced to leave the Bishopric in 1913 when increasing traffic made it difficult to continue.

20 *The Bishopric was also known as Lower West Street and Oxford Road. This picture, facing west in the opposite direction to the photograph of the market, is taken from a painting signed by local artist W.S. Russell (1849-1930). He started his business life with his father Julius as a grocer and tea merchant at 20 West Street, but his love was watercolour painting.*

– Piries Place, Pump Alley or Talbot Lane and Morth Gardens – are remains of ancient rights of way that led into the marketplace from the rear of the burgage areas.

In 1449 Henry VI granted permission for a weekly market and two fairs to be held in the area now called the Bishopric, which was part of the outlier of Marlpost. The fairs were to be held over three days, one in the week before Whitsun, and the other one in November. The Archbishop of Canterbury, anxious to cash in on a good scheme, was only too pleased to enrich the church coffers in this way.

In time fairs for horses, sheep and cattle became established at different times of the year. Welsh drovers brought their cattle 'on the hoof' over the North Downs along well-established routes to Horsham. These links may have become established because the de Braose family owned estates in Wales. Cattle were also needed for the London market and Horsham appears to have benefited from its proximity to the capital. The fairs and markets appear to have been very successful and profitable, increasing both the revenue and status of the town. They were the chief means of trade and exchange, for it was on these occasions that most contact with the outside world took place.

Evidence of the growing importance of Horsham on a national scale is indicated in 1295, when two borough representatives were

21 *The 15th-century building once called Glaysher's was formerly in Middle Street.*

summoned to the King's Parliament (each burgess had two votes for electing two of their number), and in 1322, when Horsham supplied one armed footman for the war in Scotland, in common with other towns.

Between 1250 and 1370 the Crown made occasional purchases of iron objects from the Horsham area. Normally the iron was worked up locally for agricultural uses, for it was comparatively costly, but when the occasion demanded it was used for other requirements, such as providing essentials for warfare. The earliest recorded export from the area dates from 1327, when 1,000 horseshoes were sent from Roffey to Newcastle-on-Tyne for £4 3s. 4d., with 5s. for the cost of transporting them down to Shoreham. Another export, in 1338, was a consignment of 6,000 arrows from Horsham to the Tower of London.

Additional evidence of trade comes from 13th-century pottery found on the site of Causeway House, indicating trading links with France and implying that a person of status owned the property or lived there. There are references to merchants trading in Horsham: in 1254 there were two drapers, Alan and Randall, and Walter Randolf was selling cloth and wine in 1270. He was typical of many of the merchants who became burgesses in that he was clearly wealthy, owning four houses, a mill and three acres of land in addition to land elsewhere. He was also one of the first burgesses to represent Horsham at Parliament. By 1296 leading burgesses owned more than one burgage and they expressed their wealth and status by investing their profits in buildings that they then rented out to others, often craftsmen and traders. The evidence of the Subsidy Rolls of 1296, 1327 and 1332, which were a means of raising money by the Crown, is that control of the borough was being concentrated into fewer hands, as burgesses owned more than one plot.

These earliest Subsidy Rolls are a useful source for early livelihoods – William the cooper, William the skinner, Thomas the baker and Thomas the glover are just some of the names and occupations listed in them. Representatives at Parliament included Nicholas the smith, who fulfilled one of the essential crafts in the local economy, Peter the turner and Roger Spicer. As Horsham grew in size and prestige the trend for country people to send their sons to Horsham as bound apprentices increased, and the related growth in manufacturing contributed to the town's wealth.

Some people used part of their homes for commercial activities, especially those that lived nearest to the town centre. The shop was at that time an integral part of the domestic dwelling. A horizontal counter was let down to project out into the street, with an unglazed opening above where craftsmen worked and displayed their wares. Glaysher's was a building in Butcher's Row containing two shops and dates back to the late 15th century. At the back of each shop was a small hall or 'smoke' bay open to the roof where smoked meat or pies may have been made. In 1967 the site was needed for redevelopment so this medieval building was dismantled and re-erected at the Weald and Downland Open Air Museum.

A collection of medieval green glazed pots, jugs, a goblet with a cover, some wooden items and a silver coin of Edward I was unearthed in West Street in 1867. This collection is known as the 'Horsham Hoard' and is on display at the Horsham Museum. The range and diversity of shapes of the pots and jugs indicate widespread use. They are quite decorative, suggesting that they were used at table or served to persons of wealth or importance. It is possible that different shaped jugs were used to hold different drinks

– ales, wines or beers. There were many inns, taverns and beer shops in Horsham, encouraging a bustling social scene on fair – and market – days.

A downside to the increased prosperity of the town was crime. In 1248 there is the first record of punishment of a Horsham criminal. The Assize Rolls of Lewes for 1261-2 record, 'Borough of Horsham, Hugh de la Denne and Alice wife of John Le Peck killed the said John husband of the said Alice and Hugh and Alice fled. Therefore they are outlawed.' It seems likely that prisoners were detained in a small lock-up in the Market House, which was on the site of the present Town Hall.

Horsham's position and economic success led to its eventually becoming an assize town. The decision to include Horsham as part of the system of administering justice on a national

22 *A doll, dating c.1780, with a wooden head and leather arms and legs, was found under the floor boards of Glaysher's together with some marbles and a comb.*

scale enhanced its prestige still further in the county. The first assizes, where serious cases were heard before a High Court judge, occurred in Horsham in 1306, when 22 criminal and 57 civil cases were heard. Coroners' courts have been held in the town since the early 14th century and in 1362 the Court of Quarter Sessions began. These were local courts held four times a year by the justices of the peace, who, as keepers of the peace, had administrative and criminal responsibilities.

The town benefited when the courts were in progress for many visitors came in with money to spend. The arrival of a judge and his retinue on the circuit created a stir, with all the attendant ceremonial proceedings. The vicar preached a sermon on the first evening and all available inns and taverns were crammed full with visitors. Some of these were officials and litigants, others were keen to join in the 'fun' or make a quick monetary profit in some way or other. Excitement was heightened by the fact that many punishments ended in the death penalty. Hanging was common. Horsham Common to the north of the town witnessed many such procedures. Eight of the felons found guilty in 1306 were sentenced to be hanged.

23 *The old entrance to Morth Gardens was accessed by an archway between nos 12 and 13. The footpath marked the boundary between the borough and church land. It was named after a carpenter, John Morth, who built three cottages there for his daughters.*

24 *The town grew up at the lowest point where the river could be crossed between rising ground on either side. The earliest crossing was likely to have been near the church. The view of the tower and spire, the principal feature of the church, has recently been partially obscured by the addition of a vestry.*

The people of Horsham were under the authority not only of the burgesses and bailiffs but also of the church, which was very powerful in the Middle Ages. Even the lord of the manor was anxious to be on favourable terms with the ecclesiastical authorities. De Braose decided to build a stone church sometime in the early part of the 12th century, the characteristic action of a Norman lord wishing to impose his authority. The Normans used stone because this was more permanent than wood and such buildings symbolised power and stability. The church was built close to the crossing point of the river Arun by Denne Road. It may have been built on the site of a Saxon church but no traces of such a building have been found. A century later the Norman building was practically demolished. It may have become too small for the growing population of Horsham. By about 1247 the rebuilding was completed in the Early English style and is clear evidence of Horsham's improved status and economic prosperity. St Mary the Virgin is Horsham's only Grade I listed building and is one of the finest churches in the Weald.

The church was the most substantial building in Horsham and a sharp contrast to the cramped and smelly homes of most of the parishioners. It was deliberately designed to be a visual display of the church's power within the community. It

25 *The left-hand side of this timber-framed building with Horsham slab roofs in North Street is dated pre-1550. A 1545 inventory referred to the 'capital messuage there called the Brothered house lying in the North street with the kitchen, stable and garden'. The vyse, or outside compartment, and oriel window were built to accommodate a staircase when the open hall was floored in. The building now accommodates offices for the PMMS consultancy group.*

dominated the town in its prime position, close to the centre of commerce in the marketplace. There were no health, leisure or art centres in those days and so the church was the best place to conduct civil and legal business and hold other gatherings. This may explain the presence of seats in the porch. It fulfilled a social and administrative role as well as being the centre of worship.

It was also at this time that John de Braose granted the advowson (the right of presentation by a patron to a vacant church or benefice) of the parish church to the struggling Benedictine nunnery the de Braoses had founded at Rusper in 1170. This gave the nunnery the income from the great tithes. The tithe was an annual payment of one-tenth of the yearly produce and stock of the land, which was payable by parishioners for the support of the parish church and its clergy. They were paid 'in kind', through crops, lambs, calves, wool, fish or honey. There were

two types of tithe – great and small. The great, or 'rectorial', tithes were payable to the rector of the parish, or in this instance, Rusper Nunnery. These tithes comprised the corn, other grains, hay and wood.

The small tithes, known as 'vicarial' tithes, were paid to the vicar and comprised all other tithes. In 1231 Roger of Wallingford was the first named vicar appointed in Horsham. As the parish was large, covering an area of 16 square miles, and including what are now the separated parishes of Roffey, Southwater and Broadbridge Heath, three assistants were appointed to help the vicar.

The influence of the church was also seen in Horsham in another way. It was not unusual for wealthy people to found chantries. The primary object was to maintain a priest to pray for the soul of the departed founder. The chaplain derived his stipend from lands and rents bestowed on the chantry. In Horsham the founding of chantries is important as evidence of a wealthy class of individuals. A chantry was provided in 1307 by one of the first parliamentary representatives, the burgess Walter Burgeys. He may have had mixed motives for doing this. Perhaps his lifestyle had been such that he was afraid of the pains of purgatory or maybe he wished to perpetuate his memory within the town. Perhaps he imagined he could buy his way into heaven? The chapel lay on the north side of the church, and was later integrated into the church building and is known today as the Holy Trinity Chapel. The priest who celebrated divine service daily for the souls of Walter Burgeys and his family officiated first in the church porch until a chapel could be built, and so it came to be known as 'the chauntrie in the porch'.

In 1447 licence was granted to Richard Wakehurst to found a chantry north of the chancel, in memory of his friends Henry and Mary Boteler. It was known later as the Roffey (Roughey) Chantry and today as St Nicholas Chapel. The corporate desire and ability to provide poor relief was seen in the foundation of the Brotherhood or Guild of Horsham, in 1457-8, in the south aisle of the 13th-century chapel of St John the Baptist. The role the church played in caring for these people was valued in the town and showed that the church

26 *The Causeway has known many famous and distinguished people in its time, including Horsham-born Hammond Innes, the action adventure writer, who lived at 18 Causeway as a boy in the 1920s and attended the Causeway Preparatory School. The Chantry was home to Sir Hartley Shawcross, Chief Prosecutor for the UK before the Military International Tribunal at Nuremberg.*

embraced the needs of the destitute as well as the rich. The Brotherhood consisted of a master, four wardens and some parishioners, among who were an Agate, a Lintott, a Michell, a Potter and a Waller, all names that are well known in Horsham through the centuries. The poorhouses that were built in Normandy, later to be replaced by almshouses, were probably run by the Brotherhood 'to be let to the poore without anie rente taking for the same', according to an inventory of 1548.

One of the grantees for the founding of the Brotherhood was Thomas Hoo. He was an ancestor of Anne Boleyn and his wife's grandmother was a former widow of Thomas, Lord de Braose, whose monument is also in the church. He was M.P. for Horsham three times and twice represented Sussex in Parliament. He owned lands in Roffey, Horsham and Itchingfield. Thomas Hoo's canopied tomb was erected in the church soon after his death in 1486.

Horsham does not appear to have been affected particularly badly by the Black Death of 1348, and was considered important enough to be recorded on the Gough Map, one of the earliest maps of the country, which was drawn up c.1360. As its reputation grew during the medieval period, due to its status as a borough and market town, it became an increasingly desirable place in which to settle. Many inhabitants were prosperous enough to build impressive and substantial timber-framed houses. A number of these remain today, especially in the Causeway. Easily available local materials were used for building but extensive use was made of the local sandstone – the remnants of the prehistoric lakeshore – which has been quarried in the parish since at least the 14th century and was useful for the purpose because it could be split into thin sheets, unlike some other stones. As a practically indestructible material, 'Horsham slabs' or 'stones' were used for roofs and floors on many buildings. They were used, too, for paving streets and can still be seen today in parts of the Causeway. E.V. Lucas observed in the *Highways and Byways of Sussex* that the weather 'works like a great artist in harmonies of moss, lichen and stain' on the large, grey flat slabs. These gained a wide reputation and were used, not just in Horsham, but in many other parts of Sussex as well.

THREE

Tudor Tales

The political ambitions of the powerful Howard family during the Tudor years gave to Chesworth Manor a prominence on the national scene that it had not possessed before and never achieved again. The family were at the centre of court affairs for many years. The 3rd Duke was uncle to Anne Boleyn and Catherine Howard, the two Queens of Henry VIII that were beheaded. The Howards never regarded Chesworth as their main power base – this was reserved for their East Anglian estates – but members of the family stayed on occasions as it was relatively close to the London court scene. The Dowager Duchess Agnes, widow of the 2nd Duke and known as a stiff-necked, testy and old-fashioned person, visited on occasions. She was charged with looking after her step-granddaughter, Catherine Howard, who lived at Chesworth during her adolescence.

Catherine was about twenty when she was married in July 1540 to the King, who was some thirty years her senior. She was in essence a pawn in the hands of senior members of her family. Had she behaved in the manner expected of a Queen by Henry, she would have kept her head, but her alleged conduct with young men was her undoing. Allegations involving her music teacher who lived in Horsham, Henry Mannock, were included in the charge against her. Her short time as Queen ended abruptly with her execution in February 1542, and this provoked a national crisis. The Howards were disgraced. Both the 3rd Duke and the Dowager Duchess were imprisoned in the Tower of London. The eldest son of the 3rd Duke, the Earl of Surrey, was executed on charges of treason in 1547 and the manor passed for a short time into the hands of the Seymours, political rivals of the Howards. Thomas Howard, the 4th Duke of Norfolk, was executed for his links with Mary Queen of Scots and his complicity in the Ridolfi plot of 1572.

A 1549 Chesworth inventory records that this was a substantial mansion with over 20 rooms and other functional outbuildings. Generally everything was suffering from neglect and the former splendour of the manor in the days of the de Braose family had faded away. The items listed in the following inventory are typical: 'Tappestry verye old and sore woryn', ' borde carpets and fote carpets of Turkye worke, olde and woryn'. 'A banner of sylke with flowers of gold' in the chapel 'was ragged'. The Bishop of Chichester leased the house for five years, and an inventory at his death in 1582 describes Chesworth as a target for vandals and thieves.

Despite the varying fortunes of Chesworth there were links between the estate and Horsham that provided employment and business for local people. In 1541 burgess Richard Bishop married Elizabeth Foys (Voices). She was a member of a prosperous Horsham family and daughter of the keeper and under-steward of the house and park, fellow burgess Henry Foys. Peter Ravenscroft, a widower who originated from Cheshire, also married into the Foys family when he wed Jane Foys, Henry's widow. Following her death he then married Jane's daughter-in-law, Elizabeth Foys, in 1569. Peter Ravenscroft was Master of the Horse to two magnates, the Duke of Somerset and the Duke of Norfolk, and died a wealthy man, having bought, as part of his assets, land that belonged to the Duke of Norfolk. These marriages between families of social standing were probably all 'arranged', and normally involved settlements of land and property to the mutual benefit of those involved.

In 1602 the most distinguished of the Howards' servants, Sir John Caryll, serjeant-in-law, who lived nearby at Warnham and had kept a check on the manor and estates, took a long lease on Chesworth. Partial demolition and rebuilding was done to convert the place into a farmhouse. Thomas Eversfield, a member of the family who made their fortune from ironworks in Surrey, Sussex and Kent, chose to reside at Horsham in 1604 and probably used much of the masonry to rebuild his premises on Denne Hill. From then until well into the 18th century the Eversfields were to play a key role in the politics of the town.

During the turbulent period of the 1530s one beneficial act of Henry VIII's Chancellor of the Exchequer, Thomas Cromwell, was his order that every parish priest was to 'kepe one boke or registere wherein ye shall write the day and yere of every weddyng, christenyg, and burying'. This is a key documentary source for Horsham, especially for family historians. The registers begin at 1540. There are also many Tudor wills and inventories which give details of possessions, buildings and trades. The Coroners' Records and the Calendar Assize Rolls of Elizabeth I provide details of the harsher side of life. So, from now on, enough written evidence survives to allow a more detailed picture of the lives of the townspeople to be made.

Entries for members from families across the social spectrum are included in the registers. In the earlier years there are entries relating to the members of the household of the Duke of Norfolk, or of the Earl and Countess of Arundel.

27 *Chesworth by William Penstone, from* A History of the Castles, Mansions and Manors of Western Sussex *by Elwes and Robinson (1876). Nothing remains of the original house, which was on a site south of the present house where the river formed the south part of a moat. Over the centuries there has been much rebuilding, and very little remains today of earlier buildings, which included a medieval open hall.*

28   *A postcard of a Horsham residence, postmarked during the Edwardian days of 1905; street and people unidentified. Families have lived and worked in Horsham for generations although the reason for taking this group is unknown.*

29   *The church displays the only remaining Norman architecture in Horsham. The tower and the north-west corner, including the round-headed doorway on the north wall, are the oldest parts of the building. Adjacent to the churchyard is Flagstones, roofed in Horsham stone slates and part of a medieval timber-framed open hall house. In 1805 one of the tenants was a Quaker, Samuel West, who wrote a poem called* Reflections among the Tombs in Horsham Churchyard.

One such entry reads: '1543. The x daye of the same monthe was crystened Mistres Elysabeth Howerd the daughter of Lord Thomas Howerd.' There are also records of immigrants. Many people had been forced to leave France because of religious persecution in late medieval times and some had settled in the town, bringing their skills in iron and glass working. The baptism of a bastard of a 'Frenche wenche' is recorded in November 1550. A Flemish shoemaker – an old man – was buried in 1551.

The register of burials gives a vivid, and sometimes poignant, picture of how people met their death. Infant mortality was high and occasionally the burial of a baby is recorded on the same day as a baptism or just a few days later. Many died young, before they could marry. Accidental deaths, related to water or work or transport, feature intermittently. In 1550 Robert Johnson, servant to the Lord Chancellor the Earl of Southampton, was drowned and buried whilst staying at Chesworth. In 1582 an accident befell John Rowe, who was 'killed with ye fall of a May pole, as it was setting up'. Inhabitants were vulnerable to outbreaks of plague, smallpox and other diseases. In 1557 there were 24 burials in November alone, and in the next two years influenza epidemics took their toll with over 200 deaths – a sombre record of the frailty of life in those days. Plague hit the town in 1560, a year with 111 recorded deaths, and again in 1574. Some people lived to an old age and this was commented upon, perhaps because it was comparatively rare. In December 1555 Margaret Lydseye, a widow reputed to be of the age of 104, was buried.

The coroners' inquests record sudden deaths, some of which were self-inflicted, while others were accidents or results of disputes. In 1504 there was a fatal fight between two Horsham men: Arnold Bulner, harper, killed William Pyfolde, tailor, when he hit him on the head with his staff, either by mischance or in self-defence. In 1534 a poor woman named Elizabeth

Swifter, whose master was Henry Michell, a tanner and grandson of John Michell of Stammerham, drowned herself at Castle Field. In 1551 Elizabeth, the 13-year-old daughter of Thomas Michell of Hills, died accidentally when she left a parlour with 9d. in her left hand and a bread knife and cheese in her right hand. Climbing defective stairs in 'le superiore parte' of the hall, she fell on the knife, which gave her a mortal wound on the left side of her neck. In 1556 a troubled Stephen Parson hanged himself in his house with a penny halter.

The official records of criminal trials at Sussex assizes held under Elizabeth I are found in the Calendar Assize Rolls and record details of charges and sentences. Crimes by Horsham inhabitants cover a whole gamut of offences, including assault, burglary, theft, murder, coinage, desertion from the muster, recusancy – recusants were Roman Catholics who did not attend the services of the Church of England as required by law – and vagrancy, the laws of which criminalised large numbers of poor, homeless and unemployed people. Vagrancy became a great problem in Tudor times. The increasing population, and closure of the monasteries which had looked after many of the poorest, meant there was an increase in 'vagabonds'.

In 1579 Richard Sharpe, charged with having assaulted his wife, broken her neck and thrown her into a pond, was fortunate to be found not guilty. Those that were accused of a crime might be branded, whipped or placed in the stocks or pillory, all punishments meted out in public in the Carfax and marketplace. John Sharpe, a husbandman of Horsham, was whipped for stealing a pair of hose in 1583. Elizabeth Tydye, widow, was whipped for petty larceny in 1601. Pregnant women were sometimes fortunate and let off with a charge.

A number were condemned to hang for crimes that would be considered minor today. They included Edward Bullenger and John Williams, labourers of Horsham, for burglary in

30 *The Carfax was the site for the stocks, pillory and whipping post, where offenders were placed for public ridicule. Stones and garbage were thrown at them. The stocks seen today are a replica. Bull-baiting also took place here and continued until about 1813. The bull was tethered to a ring in the west side of the Carfax. It was said that bull-baiting improved the flavour of the meat, which was sold by auction in Butcher's Row.*

1530, Thomas Chalcroft, labourer of Beeding, for burglary at the house of Horsham innkeeper Thomas Turner in 1581, and Chris Fletcher of Beeding, labourer, who burgled the house of gaol-keeper Nicholas Lintott in 1589, stealing 23 pieces of pewter and a brass pot.

A proportion were able to claim benefit of clergy. If a prisoner could read from the Bible he was declared to be in holy orders and so could not be hanged for a crime. The reasoning was that the clergy were taught to read, therefore if a person could read they must be members of the clergy! A person claiming benefit of clergy

was branded on the thumb to prevent him claiming again. Edward Topsell, labourer, having been found guilty of stealing a purse containing 27s., was given benefit in 1552.

The first record in the parish registers of a prisoner's burial comes with the entry in 1541 of Richard Sowton of Nuthurst for coining money. He was hanged at Horsham. Prisoners were kept in a gaol whilst they were awaiting trial and it seems that Horsham had the county gaol by this time, although successive sites were to be used. In 1578 a man was hanged at Southwark for murdering the Horsham gaoler

31 *Stan Parsons, affectionately known as 'Mr Horsham', kept a newsagent's shop in the Carfax for 43 years, raised money to buy a Spitfire in the Second World War, was a founder member of the Horsham Society in 1955 and an independent town councillor. 'Stan's Way', a pedestrian route linking East Street with Pirie's Place and opened in December 2000, is named after him.*

in a field there. The first gaol was probably behind a private house on the north-east side of the Carfax to the west of North Street. In 1584 Richard Lintott, cooper, left his brother Nicholas 'the great howse sometime the Gaile howse with a garden'. In 1589 Nicholas entered into a covenant with the High Sheriff of Sussex, Thomas Pelham, to receive, detain and deliver prisoners in return for fees the prisoners had to pay for board and lodging. His duty as gaoler was to hold the suspected criminals and produce them at the assizes and carry out any executions and judgements. Combined with the gaol was a House of Correction for the idle and disorderly, and for both of these the parish had some

financial responsibility. Churchwarden accounts record the taxes levied.

Nicholas Lintott was indicted eight times for 'negligent escapes' of prisoners from the gaol. He was normally fined, but it may well have been to his financial advantage, by accepting bribes, to allow prisoners to escape. He also owned a taproom nearby and supplemented his income by charging for drink. Some of the prisoners died in gaol whilst awaiting trial, others were joined by their wives; a number of women gave birth, and a few prisoners were detained indefinitely because they could not afford to pay their debts. The surroundings in which they lived were squalid and unpleasant, and disease was rife. At the time the authorities tolerated these conditions because it was thought they might act as a deterrent.

A number of inventories for Horsham survive from 1610, seven years after the death of the last Tudor monarch, Elizabeth I. They offer glimpses of accommodation and show that a specialisation of rooms was becoming a feature, especially in yeomen homes. The inventory of Robert Tredcroft, yeoman, for the *Red Lion*, is dated 1611. He was a prosperous man owning several properties besides holding a life interest in the *Red Lion*, which stood at the corner of the Carfax and West Street and was part of a burgage plot that is now occupied by Ottakar's bookshop. This was a commodious building, nearly 46 feet long on the Carfax side and over 20 feet long down the West Street side. There were beer and wine cellars, 17 rooms, and various other rooms that may have been in outbuildings. Listed were two parlours, hall, buttery, kitchen, chambers, lofts, garrets, brewhouse, milkhouse, stables and barns. Robert Tredcroft also possessed 26 bedsteads, some of which were bedsteads with curtains and others the simpler truckle beds, as well as a selection of feather and flock beds, all provided to cater for visitors who used the premises.

The range of goods that wealthy people owned is shown by both inventories and wills. Both give intriguing details of personal possessions, the wills indicating what was valued highly. One such will is that of Robert Richardson of Horsham, who died in 1541 although it is not known where he lived. His bequests included gold rials (coins first minted in Edward IV's reign) an angel noble (a gold coin), beds with coverlets, blankets, bolsters and pillows, pairs of sheets, a chest and all the hangings in his chamber, a marble-coloured coat, black hood, best gown and cap, buckskin doublet, two cows and two sheep.

Some people, possibly mindful of the need to seek divine forgiveness, left bequests in their wills for the church, perhaps for repairs or for buying items such as candles. George Foys, brother of the previously mentioned Henry Foys, left a bequest in his will of 1521 towards 'ye bying of a white sute of vestments' and Alice Sharpe, in her will of 1540-1, wished her best towel to be made into an altar cloth.

One of the most important Tudor wills to affect Horsham was that of Richard Collyer, citizen and successful mercer in London. Apprenticed to the Mercers' Company, he acquired his wealth from overseas trade, and by the time he died in 1533 had attained the position of Warden. It was due to his vision and wealth that the town had its first school, for 'to keep a Free Scole in Horsham in the Countie of Sussex where I was borne' was one of his bequests. This oldest surviving school in Sussex was born of family tragedy, for if Collyer's original intentions had not been thwarted by their untimely deaths, his fortune would have gone to his children.

32 *A fine view of the east window of the parish church and two buttresses at each side. An old vicarage once stood in the north-east corner of the churchyard, close to the vestry.*

In his will Richard Collyer stipulated that 60 Horsham scholars were to be brought up and educated in a grammar school. The money to do this was to be provided by the proceeds of the sale of one of his London homes. The financial provision for a foundation for payment of salaries and repairs to a new school building was to be assured by the handing over of his second great London house to the Mercers as trustees. In 1540 a messuage and garden deliberately near the church was purchased on a site which is occupied today by St Mary's Church School. Scholars entered the new school in 1541 and for the first time education in the town was available on a secular basis, taking the monopoly away from the church and providing a way to take the poor boy from the shop to the university. Richard Collyer's widow, Katherine, left money for a close, known as Little Horsham, adjoining the school where the scholars relaxed playing cricket, running games and archery.

Richard Collyer's ideas for the governing of the school continued from 1541 to 1889. The government was left to the vicar, aided by his churchwardens and 'honest parishioners', who were to choose the scholars, the Master and the Usher. The Company confirmed the appointment of the Master and Usher, paid their salaries and repaired the school. Towards the end of the Tudor period the parish elected two 'Overseers' annually. Only 20 years after the building of the premises, the schoolhouse was 'in ruin and decay' and the Company was obliged to pay for repairs.

The first Master of the school was Richard Brokebanke. It was his responsibility to 'teach and applye the scholleres to grammer and the latten tongue', so he devised a curriculum that consisted of Latin for eight hours a day, six days a week and 40 weeks of the year – a normal timetable for scholars being prepared for entry into Oxford or Cambridge universities. It was, however, a strict regime for the pupils, who were

33 *The Usher's House at Collyer's School drawn by D. Hurst. The original schoolhouse was converted from an existing timber-framed building that was extended in the 17th century.*

34 *A mill and millpond existed in Horsham before 1231, for in that year it was ordained that Rusper Priory should receive part of a garden and a mill under the terms of the endowment of the parish church. The pond was a popular spot for a swim, especially for Collyer's boys when the school was nearby. In the 18th century water was pumped by means of a water wheel at the Town Mill and conveyed in wooden pipes up the Causeway to a reservoir in North Street.*

expected to converse in that language from an early stage of their education.

The running of the new school was at times controversial, especially when James Alleyn held the position as the fifth Master, from 1567-1617. He combined the duties and salaries of Master and Usher, started to charge admission fees and even abolished the usher's post altogether for a time. The Alleyn family enjoyed an eminent position in the town at this period. Alleyn's wife was the daughter of the surgeon to Queen Elizabeth and his brother, Matthew, was Vicar of Horsham from 1574-1605. The position as

Master was only one of the multifarious interests of James Alleyn; he was a physician, a notary public, the parish clerk and, in 1588, fearing an invasion by the Spaniards, he raised a troop of home defenders. In 1595 innovations were introduced into the school, such as a more flexible curriculum, and the Usher was instructed to 'teach the schollers to read, wright and caste accounte' to the lower half of the school. The changes found favour with many of the townspeople, for not all were desirous of sending their sons to university. Many felt that a wider, practical education would be more beneficial for boys who would take up apprenticeships and learn crafts.

Thomas Garnet was a scholar during the time of James Alleyn for a few years in the late 1580s. He came from a devout Roman Catholic family. He later became a Jesuit and was implicated in the Gunpowder Plot of 1605. Three years later he was hanged, drawn and quartered at Tyburn for attempting to spread Roman Catholicism.

35 *This likeness of Thomas Garnet was painted at the Valladolid Seminary, Spain, in 1620.*

Association with the parish church featured high in the priorities of the school, with daily services, special celebrations on feast days and catechism. Even in the 19th century the Head-master had to take into account the vicar's wishes. Initially the scholars sat in the chancel, with a special stall allocated to the Master, although they later occupied a different part of the church.

Scholars and parishioners alike would have heard some form of choral singing in the church. There may even have been a small choir by this time; there is a possible reference to this in the 1520 will of John Michell of Stammerham, who ordained that in his Chapel of Jesus (later called the Shelley Chapel and now the All Saints Chapel) the anniversary of his death should be kept and sung every month until 12 months had passed and for this 'every stipendiary preste within the foresaid church beying present have for his labour 6d. kepying two masses with note … and the parysshe clerk to have 4d. and fower singing children 4d. they be paide at the monethes ende'.

In the will of priest John Roberts, dated 1546, his 'pryck song book' was bequeathed to the church, an indication that music was by then being marked or 'pricked' out on a stave. There was also an organ, although the date when this was installed is unknown. There are no Churchwarden Accounts earlier than 1610 but there is mention in 1613 of 7s. 6d. being received for the 'Oulde Orgaine pipes'. Either the old organ was being replaced or renovated.

The confused process that was the English Reformation began as a result of Henry VIII's marriage to Anne Boleyn, the subsequent assertion of his authority and his quarrel with the Pope. Like everywhere else in the country, Horsham was affected: Rusper Priory was dissolved in 1536 and the rectorial tithes were granted to Sir Robert Southwell, Master of the Rolls, who became the lay impropriator. The patronage of the vicarage was given to the Archbishops of Canterbury.

The function of the chantry priest was suppressed in 1529 by an Act of Parliament that forbade the payment of a salary to clergy who sang masses for the souls of the dead. This must have been an unpopular move, for many people arranged for masses to be sung after their death. In 1536 Sir Roger Copley of Roffey Manor dissolved Boteler's Chantry but the church commissioners later appropriated the endowments of the chantry. In about 1541 Sir John Caryll dissolved the Holy Trinity Chantry. The estates, which included a house and at least 115 acres in Horsham, afterwards descended in the Caryll family. The Guild suffered a similar fate to the chantries: the endowments were suppressed; the property passed to the Crown and was sold between 1548-55.

Inside the church building much of the colour was obliterated. Graphic paintings on the walls – the medieval method of depicting biblical scenes to an illiterate population – were whitewashed over. This probably occurred in the

36 *Henry VIII named Horsham as a see but this was not enacted until 1968. The suffragan bishops of Horsham lived at Worth until the fourth bishop, the Rt Revd Lindsay Urwin, was consecrated Bishop in 1994 and chose to live in Horsham.*

37 *After the Dissolution the Priory was sold, with the new owners receiving the great or 'rectorial' tithes as lay impropriators. Eventually these came into the possession of the Hurst family.*

reign of Edward VI, although there are records in 1625-6 of painters being paid for 'worke in Whiting the Church'. The burning of candles and tapers that had long been a custom was similarly discouraged as this was regarded as popish and superstitious.

A brass that has survived is that of Elizabeth Foys, who married Richard Foys and was the mother of George and Henry Foys. This brass, only 17½in. high, is all that remains of twin brasses. On the death of her husband Elizabeth probably followed the custom of the time and had two brasses made, one for her husband and one for her, to be mounted when she died. Originally the effigies were at the west end of the church with the inscription: 'Here lieth Richard Foys and Elizabeth his wife, which Richard deceased the 22nd day of April, the yere 1513: o thir souls Ihu have m'cy.' The brass of Elizabeth is interesting because it represents contemporary costume, including the pyramidal form of head-dress.

Several local families in the area, of high social standing, remained Roman Catholic after the Reformation, most notably the Howards, Carylls, Coverts and Copleys, along with their servants. This encouraged those of the same faith to stand their ground, albeit often secretly, and a few lived in Horsham. In 1592 there was an incident when Anthony Copley, 'that desparate youth … in Horsham church threw his dagger at the parish clerk and stuck it in a seat'.

The removal of the chantry priests meant that there was no one left to assist the church priest who had many souls to look after in his extensive parish. His workload therefore increased. A chantry certificate for 1548 called Horsham 'a greate parishe and conteyneth in length five myles and within the same about nine hundred houslyng people and hathe no prieste but the parishe prieste to serve the Cure and minister which is verie slender to serve so greate a parishe'. Parishioners living on the margins may have used churches in nearer

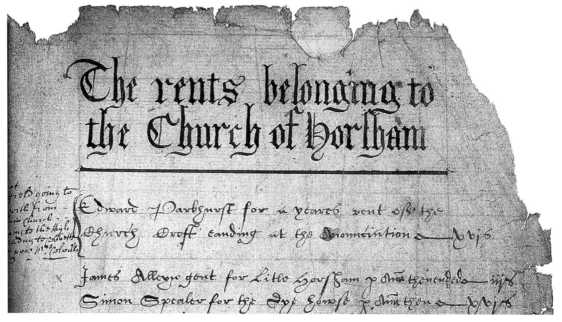

38 Portion of a folio from the Churchwarden Accounts of the rents belonging to the church, written in 1610 or 1611. The writing remains remarkably clear after nearly 400 years. The first entries are Edward Parkhurst for a year's rent of the Church Croft … 16s., James Alleyn, gent, for Little Horsham … 3s., Simon Spealer for the Dye House … 16s.

39 *St Mary's Church bells, repaired in 1921. On the left is Mr Bostock. The Revd Morley Headlam is next to him. The first peal ever rung in Sussex was a Grandsire Triples at Horsham on 11 April 1766 consisting of 5,040 changes. It took just over three hours. The ringers, drawn from the upper class of tradesmen, were Henry Weller, Thomas Lintott, William Tyler, John Foreman, Anthony Lintott, John Morth, Thomas Bristow and Thomas Aldridge. The curfew bell was rung each night until 1891.*

adjacent parishes. To accommodate the rapidly growing congregation galleries were installed in the church either in the 16th or early 17th centuries. Registers of names of those who rented them were kept in the Churchwarden Accounts.

The maintenance of the church and church-yard was an ongoing concern and some people left bequests in their wills for church works, such as repairs to the steeple or the churchyard. In 1579 the Churchwarden Presentments to the Chichester Archdeaconry refer to the church steeple being in a state of decay, with broken gutters of lead and pavements, and the church-yard being 'unrepaired'. There was a church clock and chimes that appear to have been a continual source of expense. Regular payments were made for ropes, 'oyle', 'wyer' and 'mending of ye chimes'.

Another familiar sound to parishioners was the pealing of the church bells at services and daily curfew. A bell foundry existed in the Normandy and it appears to have been very prosperous both in Tudor and Stuart times. At the beginning of the 20th century as many as 90 bells cast at the bell house were still in existence in Sussex. Horsham's 'greate bell' was recast in 1557, and in 1600 a new frame had to be built for all the bells, which numbered five at this time. A tragic accident occured in 1615, during a storm, when lightning damaged the tower and a maid, Elizabeth Strood, was killed at the belfry door.

Richard Eldridge, who came from the Eldridge foundry in Wokingham, Berkshire, worked the Horsham foundry from 1612. He ran such a successful business, dealing with many Sussex churches, that the bell house had to be enlarged or rebuilt in 1616. He paid an annual rent of 10s. to the churchwardens from 1610-22. Bells cast at this foundry carry the inscription 'Our hope is in the Lord, R.E.'. In c.1623 the Eldridge connection with the town ended when Richard's son Bryan moved away and established another foundry at Chertsey, where bells were cast for Horsham in 1633, 1645 and 1652.

By the 16th century Horsham had begun to develop other specialised trades, reflecting the high social and economic status of many of the residents of the town. Records mention an armourer, a pewterer, barber-surgeons, a cutler, a painter, a glover, a pinner, a pointer (lace-maker), a hat dresser and a glassmaker. There is also mention in the burials of four glass carriers who were possibly quarriers – people who made 'quarries' or 'quarrells', which were small diamond-shaped pieces of glass. There may have been a glasshouse in the neighbourhood of Horsham, probably on the north side, but the main centre for this was further west in the Kirdford-Chiddingfold-Loxwood area.

The town was economically self-sufficient and a large proportion of the inhabitants worked as agricultural labourers, looking after the crops and livestock. Mention of a shepherd indicates that sheep farming was practised in the parish. Many worked in occupations connected with livestock, as butchers, curriers, tanners, saddlers, shoemakers, weavers, fullers, dyers, clothiers, tailors, drapers, bucketmakers, blacksmiths and buttermen. The extensive woodlands around Horsham, which were managed and coppiced to meet the wide-ranging demands on supplies, meant that others worked in trades associated with wood and timber. Many of the same names practising the same crafts appear down the generations and often sons and daughters married into families working in the same or related spheres of activity.

The leather trade had been established in the area from early medieval times and was important, with at least 10 tanners recorded in Tudor times. Tanneries tended to be sited away from the town centre because there was always an unpleasant odour associated with the business. There was a site towards the west of Horsham, dating from medieval times, which gave the name to Tan Bridge and Tan Fields. The Pancras family were 16th-century tanners who lived near Tan Bridge. The Wallers were butchers and tanners and it is possible that Waller's Cross, which was at the junction of West Street and the Bishopric in 1543, may refer to a tannery. One advantage of Horsham being a busy market town meant that there was a ready supply of animals 'on the hoof' whose hides could be sold on to the tanners. The availability of plentiful supplies of oak bark and water locally meant the work could be developed successfully and the tanning industry continued until the early 20th century.

Another long-established trade was that of brewing. There were always plenty of beershops, not all of them licensed, to supply the needs of the people, especially on market and fair days. Many households brewed their own beer from their own hops but there were five specialist brewers who prospered in the town in 1538 through supplying the many inns, such as the *Chequer* and the *George*. Robert Tredcroft, in addition to the *Red Lion*, owned the *Anchor*, in Market Square. His son, also Robert, continued the trade of his father and was a vintner and innkeeper.

Stone quarrying and brickmaking continued to play a small yet significant part in the local economy. Many Horsham men were stone-healers or worked in the quarries. Marlpost had at least three quarries, but there was also quarrying at Shortsfield, Chesworth, Horsham Common and Stammerham. The wealthy Michell family owned Stammerham quarry where several generations of Feists leased and worked the stone.

40 *George Jupp was a thatcher and a member of the volunteer fire brigade.*

41 *The Carfax, showing the War Memorial between the Bandstand and the Queen Victoria Jubilee Fountain. This fountain became a traffic hazard and was moved in 1947. It was later re-erected but moved again in 1993 to its present position in Charts Way. A Horsham Brewery lorry is delivering at the Stout House.*

42 *The peaceful scene today of Hammer Pond belies the activity of Tudor times. St Leonard's Forest was part of the 'Black Country' of Tudor England. It was a busy, noisy and dirty place. Great furnaces that burned continuously for weeks lit up night skies. The noise from the mighty tilt hammers at the forges was incessant and dominating.*

Timber had always been used as the primary building material, but brickmaking began to develop during a period of building expansion after 1560. Those with the wealth to afford them increasingly incorporated bricks and tiles into homes. Brickworks were dotted all over Horsham, usually on sites where they were to be used in a building or on the Common, where there was available wasteland. There is a record of the burial of one Henry Soche, brickmaker, in 1555. Bricks were made from the local sands and clays. Bundles of faggots consisting of the 'lop and top' of felled trees and brushwood were used to fire the kilns.

Horsham benefited from the Wealden iron industry that had acquired national importance by the 1540s, reaching its peak in Elizabethan times. The rapid growth of London's popula-tion in the 16th century, combined with a rising prosperity, created a strong demand for iron. Cannon and shot, supplies for large ironmongers (especially those in London), and catering for the local domestic market kept the industry in business. A local man of Horsham, one George Hall, stated in 1588 that 'he had known the Forest for the space of 50 years and the ironworks he has known since the first erection and making thereof'. References to a hammerman, furnace boy, ironworks labourer and forgeman in the parish registers indicate that some of the parishioners were involved with the industry, either as smithies in the town or as workers at the nearby furnaces and forges. Activities associated with the industry, such as the provision of food, supplying raw materials, and carting away finished products, generated an income for those involved. For many people it was a profitable business with which to be associated.

During the first decades of the 16th century the old method of bloomery working was replaced by newer methods introduced by French immigrants, and St Leonard's Forest proved ideal for this industrial development. There were plentiful deposits of iron ore and abundant supplies of underwood for charcoal. Pig iron was produced in stone blast furnaces that were heated to high temperatures by charcoal and operated by water-powered bellows. The numerous streams flowing in deep narrow valleys through the forest were dammed to make hammerponds. These were created to power the bellows and drive the tilt hammers that beat out the molten iron. The majority of the ironworkers, who resided around the

forges and furnaces, and the miners and charcoal burners, who lived in the forest, would have used the facilities of Horsham, and this contributed towards the town's prosperity.

The St Leonard's Forges at Lower Beeding were in operation by 1561, possibly earlier, and the St Leonard's Furnace by 1584. These were leased to Sir John Caryll in 1601 for 60 years by Queen Elizabeth. Gosden Furnace was probably erected in 1580 and was leased out, the lessees including members of the Middleton family. In 1597 Thomas Middleton, Thomas French and Anthony Fowle were running the Dedisham Forge in conjunction with Gosden Furnace. Even closer to the centre of the town was Warnham Furnace. This was possibly in existence by the end of Elizabeth's reign and was operated by Sir John Caryll until his death in 1613. The Carylls were also involved with

43 *The earliest record of a mill at Warnham appears in a charter from the reign of Edward I dated c.1300. In the early 17th century water that collected in the millpond fed the great wheel that drove the iron-smelting bellows. After c.1660 the furnace fell into disuse. A flour mill was built to utilise the power of the water wheel and remained in use until the 1930s.*

44 *St Leonard's Forest as depicted on Christopher Saxton's map of Kent, Sussex, Surrey and Middlesex, 1575. Originally this was under royal jurisdiction. Many myths and legends associated with the forest grew up, in particular those of the dragon, 'Mike Mills Race' and Squire Paullett, the headless spectre.*

running the Knepp Furnace at Shipley for the Duke of Norfolk for over 30 years. Ironworks in the forest at Worth, that had been confiscated from the Norfolk family, were itemised in a Chesworth inventory of 1549 where it was recorded that wages of £160 were owing to workmen.

Since involvement in the iron industry could be a lucrative business for the landowners and lessees, until it declined by the end of the 17th century, it is not surprising that rivalry between ironmasters developed. There was considerable acrimony between the Gratwicks, Carylls and the Coverts. Intense disputes occurred between them, resulting in episodes of fighting and litiga-

tion. In *c.*1590 the unrest spread into Horsham, where one Thomas Marsh, with his dagger drawn, assaulted Richard Whitebread as he was going to church, and chased him into a nearby house.

The cartage of heavy supplies of timber, ore, charcoal and iron played havoc with the roads. Teams of oxen were needed to pull the great loads, cartwheels drove deep ruts in the ground and, particularly in the wet winters, the roads degenerated into thick quagmires. The need to take iron and other goods to the lucrative London market, although costly and difficult, meant that this problem was not confined to the local area. The road from Horsham to London Bridge had a notoriously poor reputation. To try to offset this Richard Collyer made provision in his will for spending £50 on the road between Horsham and Crawley and £50 on the road between Crawley and Reigate.

Each locality was responsible for maintaining the roads, but in 1555 the parish was compelled to take responsibility. The system was largely ineffective. The majority of residents in Horsham had little interest in maintaining roads for through travellers. The poor communications meant that Horsham was often isolated and bypassed when conditions were particularly bad. In 1534 an 'Acte for Amendynge of High Wayes in Sussex' was passed. Later Acts in 1584 and 1597 attempted to make the ironmasters responsible for the damage their work did to roads by contributing to their maintenance. Slag and cinders, gravel and stone were used on their upkeep. Slag has been found in the vicinity of Denne Road, pointing to the fact that it was in constant use during the iron-working period and that here at least the ironmasters had made an attempt to keep the roads operating. Nevertheless the improvements were localised, for Speed's Atlas of 1611 describes Sussex roads as 'very ill for travellers, especially in winter'.

FOUR

Friction in the Town

In the 17th century Horsham, like everywhere else, was riven by political, religious and social conflicts. James I of England ascended the throne in 1603. Both he and Charles I tried to rule independently of Parliament, which was a mistake, as they underestimated the power of this institution. Their belief in the Divine Right of Kings bred distrust and the need for parliamentary representation became more sought after as the century progressed.

In 1623 the local townspeople elected the wealthy John Middleton of Hills, J.P., to be one of their parliamentary representatives, a position he held until 1628, when Charles I dissolved Parliament and ruled without it. John Middleton was an ironmaster who had moved to the town from East Sussex just before 1600. His great-grandfather had been a servant to Henry VIII and he was an ambitious man, keen for himself and his family to make a mark within the county. One way in which he achieved this was by building a substantial mansion adjacent to the old Hills farmhouse in c.1610. This lay on a site immediately to the south of what is now Guildford Road. The fashionable Dutch gables to five bays, glazed windows and cluster of chimneys made a powerful statement, creating an impression of innovation and wealth. His election to Parliament meant that the Duke of Norfolk no longer had total control of the borough.

Churchwarden Presentments show that in the 1620s there was little trouble from Horsham people over church matters. A few were singled out for non-attendance at church, either because they were recusants or because they preferred to indulge in drinking and tippling during the time of divine service; one man took advantage of a fine Sunday to 'ted, gather and cocke hay'. But relations between the church and the people began to deteriorate in the 1630s, as A. Fletcher, in *Sussex 1600-1660, A County Community at Peace and War*, indicates. Archbishop Laud became increasingly unpopular. His programme of reform, with an emphasis on ceremony, was unpopular and brought him into open conflict with the gentry. His order that the Holy Communion table be placed behind rails in the chancel was particularly resented. Horsham parishioners were slow to carry out this order, and were reluctant to remove the seats surrounding the table that was used by communicants as requested.

Loyalties in the town became divided during the years leading up to the Civil War. Many remained indifferent – 'we wunt be druv' has always been true of Sussex people – and tried to carry on with their lives in as normal a fashion as possible without becoming involved. Some people developed strong opinions and divisions formed as politics and religion became intertwined. Collyer's School was affected when a new Master had to be appointed in 1629. Controversy broke out between the advocates of the High Church and the Puritans. The

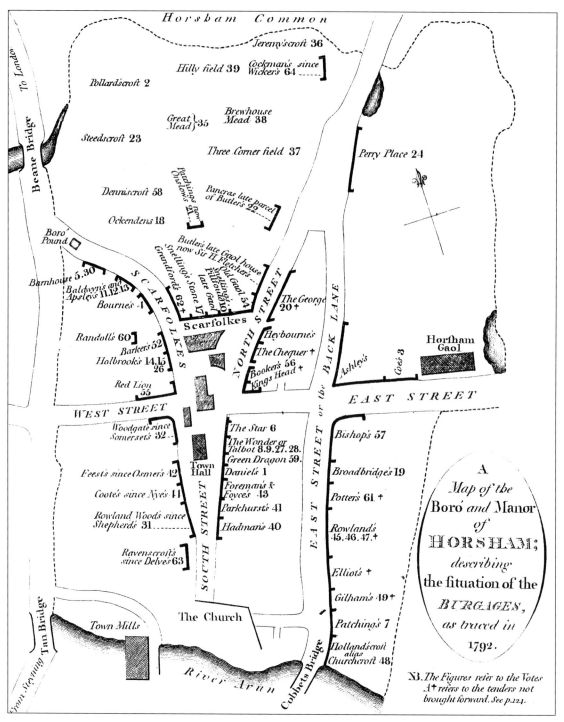

45 *Plan of the borough as traced in 1792 from a survey made in 1611. Many of the burgages were divided up and acquired several buildings, making ownership difficult to establish. Drawn by Mr S. Mitchell from Fraser's Election Cases* (1792).

46 *Making garlands announcing the coming of summer is an ancient May Day custom. Garlands were used by small girls, crowned with leaves and flowers, who went begging from door to door.*

latter, who put in Thomas Robinson, successfully opposed Archbishop Laud's choice of Edmund Pierson. The dispute, which went to Chancery, took 10 years to settle, but it singled out the Parliamentary supporters in the town, for Robinson's presentation letter included the signatures of three prominent men: Hall Ravenscroft, Nicholas Sheppard and Thomas Middleton.

Hall Ravenscroft was the grandson of the ambitious Peter Ravenscroft. He became a J.P. and M.P., signing the Solemn League and Covenant in 1640. (In the church is a beautiful black and white marble monument to Elizabeth Delves, daughter of Hall Ravenscroft, who died in 1654 during childbirth, aged around twenty-five.) Nicholas Sheppard, attorney at

law, schoolwarden of Collyer's School, and a brother-in-law of Hall Ravenscroft, was another ardent Parliamentarian. He became a member of the local committee that supported Parliamentary forces during the Civil War. In the 1640s Horsham was one of the places where the Parliamentary County Committee met.

Thomas Middleton, J.P and M.P. and the son and heir of John Middleton of Hills, was one of the most prominent men in the county on Parliament's side at the outbreak of the Civil War in 1642. He was a member of the committee for Sussex appointed to carry out the sequestration of estates from those who had sided with the King, becoming Deputy Lieutenant in 1644. When Royalist forces invaded Sussex in December 1643, however, he was forced

47 *The private estate belonged to Henry Garway Esq., Alderman of London, and was described as 'An exact and parfect surveye of the demesne's land belonging to the Manor of Tarring and lying in Horsham and Marlpost Wood lying in Shipley.' Land belonging to Horsham parishioners Michell, Lintott and Worsfold and a reference to stone quarries are recorded in the survey.*

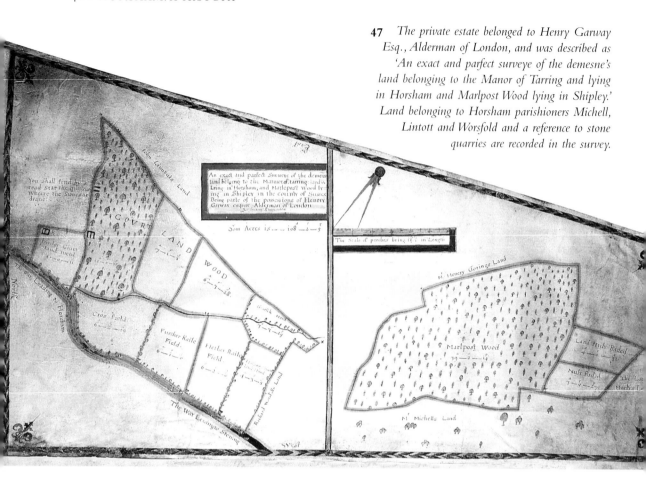

into an unprecedented position; his loyalties wavered and his support for the Parliamentarians weakened. He was accused of encouraging countrymen to resist taking up arms against the King's men. Finally losing the trust of the Parliamentarians, he was imprisoned in 1648 and his estates sequestered temporarily. Thomas Eversfield of Denne was another member of the 'new' gentry who supported Parliament and, like Middleton, was a commissioner for the sequestration of estates. When faced with the choice of siding with King or Parliament, he chose the former and was accused in 1643 of deserting the cause.

There is an amusing tale concerning Thomas Middleton related by W. Albery in *A Parliamentary History of Horsham*. It seems he was once the

involuntary cause of alarming all of London. In May 1641 the report of a plot was being read in the House of Commons, when Thomas Middleton and another gentleman, who were 'two persons of good bigness', stood up to hear better. It seems between them they

> weighed down a board in the gallery, which gave so great a crack that an alarm of fire; of the House falling; and of a malignant conspiracy, spread rapidly over the town so that a regiment of the trained bands was collected in the city upon beat of drums and marched to meet the imaginary evils.

During the 1640s an increasing number of Horsham townsfolk rejected the authority of the Anglican Church and followed the new Puritan practices, responding to the climate of the Cromwellian Parliament. Local feelings ran high. The preference for plain, austere churches, unadorned with ornaments and trappings, and for services conducted in the simplest of ways with the minimum of ritual, was at odds with High Church practice. In 1641 the communion table was removed to its 'ancient place', by order of Parliament, from its recent imposed position as an altar at the eastern end of the church behind rails. An articulate and powerful group of Puritan supporters was instrumental in the sequestration of the tithes of Horsham vicarage and in removing, in 1642, the vicar Mr Conyers, replacing him with the Puritan minister John Chatfield, a popular local preacher. It was another triumph for the Puritans in the town.

The following year the churchwardens destroyed their organ, following an order enacted by Parliament that all church organs, together with their frames and cases, were to be removed. Nine shillings was 'Rec. for the Orgin Case and for the peeces of railes.' The depiction of 'graven images', which was condemned in the Bible, in and on churches, was regarded as idolatrous by the Puritans, and it was probably during this period that the church fabric sustained other damage, with broken corbels, despoiling of tombs and the removal of stained glass windows. The Churchwarden Accounts record that 4s. 10d. was received for the brass taken out of the tombstones; John Parsons was paid 12s. for glazing the windows in 1642, 3s. in 1643 and 22s. 2d. in 1644; James Groombridge was paid £2 1s. 10d. in 1643-4 and a further 8s. in 1646 for similar work 'and carrying in and out the ladder'. The size of the sum for glazing the windows

48 *The impressive house of Denne, painted here by Dora Hurst in 1853, was built by Thomas Eversfield as a status symbol. A grand avenue of limes led from Worthing Road to the house by 1790. In c.1950 the estate was broken up and the house divided into apartments.*

49 *The shortage of coins of the realm led to shopkeepers and tradesmen minting their own coins or tokens. These were issued to customers as change that could be redeemed at a later date. Horsham had 10 tokens between 1653-69. Tokens of the 1670s, 1790s and 1920s are on display at Horsham Museum.*

50 *When the furnace at Warnham operated in the 17th century the pond was drained on a yearly cycle and ore extracted from the bottom. P.B. Shelley is said to have learnt to sail on the millpond and to have a favourite picnic spot nearby. This picture was taken soon after the floodgates, built in 1876, had given way in 1906 and drained the pond. The area was designated a Local Nature Reserve in 1988.*

suggests that these were deliberately broken so that the stained glass could be removed and replaced with plain glass. Church services were altered so that there was little music other than a metrical psalm. The Book of Common Prayer was abolished and in 1644 the Directory of Public Worship was introduced, costing the church 10d., and creating a situation that must have been displeasing to the High Church faction of the town, although this was a general order throughout the country and not specific to Horsham. Later, following the Restoration, the Prayer Book was reintroduced.

The Puritans had high standards where behaviour, drink and the keeping of the Lord's Day (Sunday) were concerned. Many were highly critical and intolerant towards those who did not conform to their standards and regarded them as immoral and spiritually decadent. The large number of inns, taverns and alehouses in the town encouraged unruly scenes and led to some individuals being singled out for punishment. In 1645 Presentments were made at the Quarter Sessions in Petworth of some who kept unlicensed alehouses or were found to be drinking and disorderly on the Lord's Day. Other shortfalls documented in church records reveal that in 1646 William Cooper was fined 12d. for missing a service on the Lord's Day, John Chapman was fined 5s. for being drunk on the Lord's Day, and John Carpenter and Richard Parsons were fined 12d. for swearing. Some people in the town regarded such fines as punitive and this created ill feeling and resentment.

The Civil War disrupted trade and the rural economy and was therefore unpopular. A petition was sent to the King at Oxford to allow for the safe passage of the Welsh cattle. The militia was disliked and people resented being forced to quarter soldiers. Inhabitants found it a struggle just to survive, especially as the decade before the war had been one of scarcity and disease and the harvests of 1646-7 were bad.

51 *Arthur Jupp, serving in the Second World War, maintains the long tradition of military involvement by Horsham men.*

Many Horsham inhabitants joined the mass protest rallies organised by the 'Clubmen', a large group of dissatisfied people who wanted a return to stability. The fear that these swelling numbers of 'stout rustics' would cause trouble led to action by the Parliamentary forces.

Horsham did not experience fighting on the scale seen by Chichester or Arundel, but one incident occurred in 1648. Tensions would have been running high between the two factions. A Parliamentary commander had reported in 1644 that he could rely on only 200 Roundheads out of a population of 509 males. There was a significant number of Royalists and these people rose up, supported by the borough bailiffs and constables, to stop Parliamentarians removing the local armoury from the Town Hall to Arundel. D. Hurst included a dramatic account in her book *Horsham: Its History and Antiquities.* The account was written by an observer who signed himself 'RT' and sent it to an official in London. It is an important source for our knowledge of events as they happened in Horsham at this time.

'RT' was probably Robert Tredcroft, the only son of the prosperous innkeeper. The town's Protestation Returns of 1642 give only one man with these initials from a list that included about five hundred male names. (A Resolution by the House of Commons the previous year had led to the taking of the Oath of Protestation by all males over 18, with a declaration that 'whosoever shall

52 *The Garden of Remembrance, on the banks of the river to the south-west of the parish church, remains a tranquil spot.*

not take the Protestation is unfit to beare Office in the Church or Commonwealth,' thereby signifying support for the state and church.) The account, dated 29 June 1648, begins with the observation that the country people are generally risen about Horsham, and protest they will fight for King and country …

> With us at Horsum we are now 500 men in arms … Our countreymen rose with one consent and two or three hundred appeared in an instant, leaving their mattocks and plowes to rescue the swords and musquets.

Robert Tredcroft was known to have held Royalist sympathies. In the charged atmosphere of the times he had been heard to declare that the King's forces 'would kill such round-headed rogues as did hold to the Parliament'. The townsfolk, having thwarted the plans of the Parliamentarians by seizing the magazine of arms, proceeded to train on Horsham Common. Some of the more influential leaders in the town fled to Lewes. They included John Chatfield, the minister, and Nicholas Sheppard. The latter was ridiculed by Robert Tredcroft who said that 'as soon as the drums beat, Captain Sheppard felt himself not well; his belly akt [ached] … and he thought to go to Lewes for some physicke'.

A clash at Knepp Castle led to action in Horsham. Early in July Parliamentarian troops under Sir Michael Livesay entered the town from the south to quell the Royalist uprising, meeting opposition in Denne Road and Park Street. The local men were no match for the disciplined Roundheads, who were a formidable force, and must have fled in panic, for there was only a handful of deaths. Graphic descriptions in the parish records state that on 5 July there was a burial of a soldier killed in the back lane, now Denne Road. On the following day three men were buried who had died fighting for their cause: Edward Filder, killed by a Roundhead thrusting his sword through the window in his house; William Baker, killed in the hop garden

53 *There were no public gardens in the town dedicated to those who had died in warfare until 1926 when Councillor Nellie Laughton, who had a preference for wearing black and white clothes, laid out the Garden of Remembrance in memory of her husband and others who had died in the First World War. Taken from the* Sunday Graphic and Sunday News *24 July 1932 entitled 'Horsham Celebrities as seen by "Matt"'.*

of Nicholas Sturt, where he had sought a hiding place; and Thomas Marshall, gentleman, killed in East Street near to Thomas Michell's door. In the following weeks the Roundheads were accused of plundering and creating disorder in the town. There was clearly a hostile atmosphere that did not augur well for the Parliamentarians living there.

An order by the Commonwealth Parliament banning weddings in church, and forcing people to be married by a J.P., was resented and unpopular. Between September 1653 and December 1657 there were over 130 marriages conducted in Horsham, with many couples coming in from the surrounding villages. Edward Michell conducted over 100 of these ceremonies. However, in deference to religious scruples the vicar, Nathaniel Tredcroft, started taking marriages in 1658.

54 *This couple was able to choose the place and clergyman for their wedding service, unlike those marrying in the 1650s. Arthur Jupp married Eileen Wright at the Congregational Church, Springfield Road, early in 1945. The church was pulled down in the 1980s when the Albion Way was being built.*

Nathaniel Tredcroft had been selected to be the vicar of the parish church in 1657 by the Sussex Commission, which appointed ministers during the Commonwealth period. He was a distant cousin of the Tredcrofts then residing in the town. Richard Cromwell, son of the Lord Protector, signed the document recording this presentation. In the citation Nathaniel Tredcroft was found to be 'a fit person to preach the gospels', and a book of his sermons was published. One book, called *Book the 4th 1685*, includes some funeral sermons and discourses

relating to the church's year and Christian behaviour. Not only did he manage to retain his position throughout all the religious changes that he encountered during his long ministry, but Land Tax records also show that he was the richest man in Horsham at his death in 1696, probably achieving this through two marriages to wives from prosperous local families.

During the 1650s a group of people in the town began to make their presence felt in a highly outspoken fashion. They were people who pursued their religion with vigour and were to attract trouble persistently for most of the remainder of the century. The members of the movement were called the Society of Friends, or the Quakers, because they 'quaked' with fervour as they prayed. Adherents ranged from lesser gentry and yeomen to blacksmiths, weavers and labourers. Many of these people were wealthy or secure enough in their livelihood to act independently and felt confident in disregarding the political and religious rulings of the day. They preferred to support a movement that esteemed honesty, literacy, fairness and prosperity. Discontent with a seemingly affluent church that demanded annual tithes and dues ran deep. There was resentment at the many ways the church could extract money from its parishioners: the payment of fines for non-attendance at services, the system of pew renting, and the ruling that a couple wishing to be married had to pay 18d. and a woman asking to be churched after childbirth 6d. (A service in the Book of Common Prayer called 'The Thanksgiving of Women after Childbirth, commonly called the Churching of Women' received a woman back into the life of the Church following childbirth.) Even if the baby died, which happened frequently, the sum of 3d. was still extracted and must have seemed particularly callous to a grieving parent.

In June 1655 John Slee, Thomas Lawson and Thomas Laycock 'declared the Truth in the open market in a powerful manner'. Later

55 *The south-east view of Horsham Church before restoration. Occasionally 'night funerals' occurred. These were elaborate, ceremonious affairs. Candles illuminated the church and the proceedings were conducted by torchlight processions. Such funerals were accorded only to the wealthy although they were watched by large crowds. The last person buried in this manner was Mrs Killick from Tanbridge in 1829.*

that same year the charismatic founder of the Quakers, George Fox, visited Horsham. He wrote in his Journal, 'From thence I passed into Sussex and lodged near Horsham where there was a great meeting, and many convinced.' Inspirational and uncompromising, Fox attracted people wherever he went on his journeys. The gatherings in Horsham marketplace were noisy affairs. Antagonistic bystanders threw stones and openly reviled the public speakers. The Friends, undaunted, did not confine their preaching to open-air meetings, but interrupted services in the church, or steeple house as they called it, trying to win over members of the congregation

and berating the vicar, John Chatfield, in the process. Their refusal to remove their hats inside the church – common practice at that time – caused further offence.

The Friends were regarded by the authorities as striking directly at the foundations of order and authority in both the church and the state and they were distrusted. Their refusal to conform resulted in local J.P.s ordering many of them to be thrown into the House of Correction or, more frequently, Horsham gaol to await trial at the next assizes. A new gaol had been built in 1640 on the north side of the Carfax, further along from the original Gaol House and gaol,

56 *The original Meeting House was built close to this site in 1693, when a burial ground was also established. It was replaced in 1786 by this building. A marriage document, dated 1765, between William Dean and Susannah Holmes is displayed in the building.*

and Thomas Laycock was the first Quaker to suffer this misfortune. Undaunted he assisted in the spread of the movement by distributing literature, which was brought in a sack on horseback into the gaol, to the 'multitudes' who came to see him. George Fox was imprisoned in Horsham gaol for three months for disrupting a church service and nearly two hundred more Quakers followed between 1655 and 1690, accepting the impoverishment and abuse that this entailed. They were kept in confinement until the next assize came round when they would be brought before the Bar. The prisoners were freed if they paid a fine, which was often excessive. Many refused in principle to do this and were reincarcerated.

The Quakers kept a book called 'A Register of Friends in Gaol at Horsham 1666-1684', which is kept at the ESRO, and this names the prisoners and gives the reasons for their imprisonment. Many were put there for refusing to take the oath of allegiance or because they would not pay church tithes, were absent from church services, attended an unlawful assembly or declined to bear arms. Ambrose Rigge, who was a leading figure in the movement in Sussex and Surrey, married his wife in the gaol. Yet his spirit was not diminished and he wrote a

number of tracts and petitions against Quaker treatment. He was discharged in 1672 by the King's Pardon after he had suffered imprisonment for 10 years and four months because he would not take the oath of allegiance.

Conditions in the gaol were unpleasant and life was harsh: a prisoner was shot dead by the tapster, Edward Michell, in 1644. The attitudes of the various gaolers towards the Quakers varied. Some treated them with abuse and cruelty whereas others were more sympathetic. Richard Luckins, the third of that name, was more leniently disposed towards the Quakers under his charge and let them out on parole. He himself was then placed in the House of Correction by angry Justices. The gaol was dark, dirty and badly constructed. Many Quakers were kept in fetters, were whipped and deprived of bedding, light and heat, even though there were at least 12 hearths in 1662, according to the Hearth Tax Returns. In November 1683 Richard Gates, a blacksmith living at Marlpost, was directed by concerned Quakers to take 20s. and visit the gaol to 'see if there be any want among the poor prisoners that did and do belong to our respective meetings and to supply them accordingly as need shall require' – something that Gates experienced himself when he was thrown into gaol. Some Quakers remembered the plight of the Friends in their wills: William Holbeam of Lewes, in his will of 1662, provided money to alleviate the sufferings of the Quakers in Horsham gaol.

At first the Quakers met informally to worship in secluded homes and barns or out in the open air, a necessary precaution once the Conventicle Act of 1664 was introduced which forbade religious assemblies of more than five people outside the auspices of the Anglican Church. They prayed together in a silence that was broken only when someone felt moved to speak. Conducted on a rotational basis, some of these gatherings occurred in and around Horsham. Quakers were well organised, with business matters conducted at quarterly and monthly Meetings, which became established at Horsham in 1668. The sexes were segregated and the opportunities that opened up for the women to lead and organise their meetings attracted many into the movement. They offered each other mutual support socially and financially, and the care of the poor and the sick always concerned them. A typical gesture occurred in 1669 when it was brought to the attention of Friends at the Horsham Men's Monthly Meeting that Ann Parsons had fallen from a horse and broken her arm. The sum of 40s. was advanced for the payment to the bonesetter.

57 *This Friends' Meeting House at Coolham, which William Penn helped to found, was attached to an isolated farmhouse. It has altered very little since the Quakers used it in the 17th century and families from Horsham attended meetings.*

58 *The Quaker Samuel Carpenter, taken from Samuel Carpenter and his descendents by Edward and Louis Carpenter. His descendants held many distinguished positions in Pennsylvania. They became, or married into, families that contained judges, ambassadors, senators, bankers, academics and State Legislature members.*

The powers of the Meetings were wide-ranging. Matters of procedure followed strict guidelines and all deliberations were recorded. For instance, John Edwards, a shoemaker in the town, was a lapsed Quaker who was the subject of a Testimony of Denial at a monthly Meeting in Horsham held on 8 January 1695. He had absented himself wholly from the society of the Quakers for some years and was publicly rebuked for being out of fellowship and required to repent. The Quakers maintained a custom of intermarrying amongst themselves and marrying 'out' was regarded with great displeasure. Marriages were normally witnessed

by a large number of relatives and Friends, even though many in the town considered them invalid.

William Penn, the son of an admiral, who became an ardent Quaker and spent many years writing and preaching, first stayed in Horsham in 1672 during his 'Journey on Truth's Account'. He and his first wife Gulielma were very active in the affairs of the Horsham and district Friends, often driving to meetings in a heavy ox-wagon whilst they resided at Warminghurst Place, near Ashington, between 1676 and 1707. Like many other Quakers Penn was imprisoned in Horsham gaol, accused of being a factious and seditious person and of holding unlawful assemblies at Warminghurst. In 1682, after Charles II had granted him the rights to the territories that were to be called Pennsylvania, William Penn sailed to America on the ship *Welcome* and founded a new colony and the city of Philadelphia for persecuted Quakers. Many Friends from Sussex, especially in the Horsham area, accompanied him.

Samuel Carpenter was a Horsham man who elected to leave his homeland and emigrate to the New World. He sailed to Barbados some time around the early 1670s. There are records of him failing to furnish men with arms and being fined as a result in 1673 and 1683. Samuel then left the Caribbean and settled in Pennsylvania, where he married and built up his business. Additionally he played a key part in the management and development of the colony in 1688, becoming one of the three Commissioners of State, and then Treasurer of Pennsylvania in 1709. The township of Horsham was built on land that Samuel had bought, the first landowner, and named after his hometown in Sussex.

There were other dissenters in Horsham, and the Restoration of the Monarchy in 1660, when the Puritan movement was overthrown, affected them all. The Corporation Act of 1661 excluded from membership of town corporations all those who were not prepared to take the sacrament according to the rites of the Church of England or take the oaths of allegiance, supremacy and non-resistance. The Test Act passed in 1673 imposed the same test upon holders of civil and military office. Dissenters and Roman Catholics alike were therefore excluded from public office, and these Acts were not repealed until 1828. Despite the attempts to discourage dissenters and strengthen the position of the Established Church, numbers of dissenters in Horsham continued to increase. One movement that was growing in popularity was the General Baptist movement. Members had, like the Quakers, been meeting in barns and houses since 1648. But, unlike the Quakers, these people did not become so isolated in their behaviour, being less puritanical and prepared to join in the social activities of the day. Yet in matters of religion they were quite different; it was their belief that baptism should be performed only to believing adults that gave them the derided term 'anabaptists.'

The most notable of the Baptists in Horsham at this time was Matthew Caffyn, a brave man of strong opinions and commanding personality, who was nicknamed the 'Battle Axe'. He regarded bishops as usurpers, had a hatred of the Roman Catholic Church and attacked the Quakers vociferously, calling them 'deceived and deceiving'. His dislike of the Quakers was matched in return by George Fox's personal animosity towards the Baptists; in 1656 Fox wrote in his Journal that 'many times [in Sussex] met with opposition from Baptists and other jangling Professors, but the Lord's power went over them'. Matthew Caffyn was not above condemning the behaviour of fellow Baptists if he thought their behaviour warranted it. He thought believers that married 'out' should be excommunicated. He was prepared to endure persecution for his faith and was imprisoned five times himself for 'unauthorised' preaching. He came from a farming family that rented farms at Broadbridge Heath and Southwater. Many meetings were held on the Caffyn

59 *In 1879 the General Baptist Meeting House became known as the Free Christian Church, and the building is now the meeting place of the Unitarian Church. Walter Dendy Sadler, the artist, was descended from a former minister, the Revd Thomas Sadler. The town's first library was based in the hall of the church. In 1893 the Minister, the Revd John J. Marten, founded the Museum Society.*

IN REMEMBRANCE OF
MATTHEW CAFFYN.
OVER SIXTY YEARS MINISTER OF THE
CONGREGATION WHICH, IN 1720-1.
ERECTED THIS MEETING HOUSE.

FIVE TIMES IMPRISONED FOR UN-
AUTHORISED PREACHING: RENOWNED
AS A BATTLE AXE AND WEAPON OF WARRE
IN DEFENCE OF HIS CONVICTIONS OF TRUTH.
BORN IN THIS TOWN 26TH OCTOBER 1628;
BURIED AT ITCHINGFIELD, 10TH JUNE 1714.

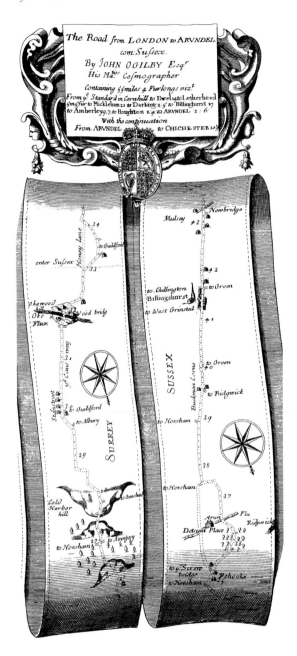

60 *The first road map, drawn on a scale of 1 inch to 1 mile in 1675, marked significant advances in cartography. The roads were depicted on scrolls or strips. Horsham is named in 'The Road from London to Arundel and Chichester', but not as a town in its own right.*

Horsham. Matthew Caffyn became the first pastor of the Baptist congregation, dying in 1714 aged 86.

The Presbyterians were another dissenting group that flourished in Horsham in the later 17th century. A notable minister was Matthew Woodman, who retired to Horsham, where 'he preached gratis' until he died in 1683. He was a descendant of Richard Woodman, one of the Sussex martyrs burnt to death in Lewes in 1557 during the persecutions of Queen Mary. Services were held in his home although a Presbyterian meeting house was built in East Street early in the next century.

In 1676, according to a religious census, there were 100 dissenters compared with 2,870 conformists in the parish, and only 30 papists. They may have been small in number but they were determined, independent people who wanted to worship in their own way. The attempt to make everyone worship in the Established Church was finally abandoned with the passing of the Toleration Act of 1689. Dissenters were allowed to worship openly although they still had to pay tithes and were barred from the establishment. By the time the century drew to a close the position of dissenters in society was more secure and during the next century nonconformity flourished in Horsham. Even the Quakers had gained the respect of their fellow men and were considered acceptable, although they were not necessarily liked, for their dignity, loyalty and probity in all aspects of their lives.

family's premises and adults were baptised in the millpond at Broadbridge on Whit Sundays – a practice that continued until 1772, when a baptistry was built in the meeting house at

FIVE

Glimpses into Eighteenth-Century Life

During the 18th century the Ingram family played a key role in the political life of the borough, dominating it for several decades. They were also the most important landowners in Horsham, owning the 'great house', of Hills. This imposing mansion had come into their possession through the marriage of Arthur Ingram, younger son of Henry Ingram, 1st Viscount Irwin, to Isabella Machell, daughter of John Machell.

John Machell had bought the Hills estate from the Middleton family. A newcomer to Horsham, he was an ambitious man, a Royalist who had the wealth and opportunity to gain political power, and he became an M.P. for Horsham in 1680, a position he held until 1700. John Machell's two sons did not survive infancy so he was determined to make a good marriage for Isabella. At the time of the marriage in 1685 Arthur Ingram, a second son, was not

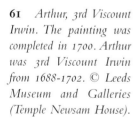

61 *Arthur, 3rd Viscount Irwin. The painting was completed in 1700. Arthur was 3rd Viscount Irwin from 1688-1702. © Leeds Museum and Galleries (Temple Newsam House).*

62 *After her husband's death Isabella, Viscountess Irwin, continued to reside at Temple Newsam supervising the education of her sons. On the marriage of her second son Rich, 5th Viscount Irwin, to Lady Anne Howard, in 1718, she moved to Windsor. © Leeds Museum and Galleries (Temple Newsam House).*

expected to succeed to the title, but on the death of his brother in 1688 he became the 3rd Viscount Irwin.

The Ingrams had made their money in textiles and their main family seat was at Temple Newsam, near Leeds. They did not choose to reside in Horsham but usually visited Hills at least once a year. After Arthur's premature death in 1702 Lady Isabella was left, aged 34, a widow. She lived to the age of 94, having outlived all her children. During her lifetime five of her nine sons became Viscounts Irwin, and three of them – Arthur, Henry and Charles – became M.P.s for Horsham. She was skilled in political manipulation, having seen at close quarters, through the affairs of her father and husband, the ways of the political world. Her fortune,

as heiress to John Machell, included Hills and the 'pocket' borough of Horsham, which was valuable to the family as a source of income from patronage. Throughout her long life Lady Isabella exerted a powerful influence over her family, particularly in the choice of spouses and in financial matters, as she attempted to mend losses resulting from the bursting of the South Sea Bubble in 1720.

In the early part of the century Charles Eversfield of Denne, M.P. for Horsham from 1705-10 and 1713-41, and for Sussex from 1710-13, was in undisputed control of the borough. By this time burgage holders had four Parliamentary votes, two for the county and two for the borough. The early contested elections in the century, those of 1701, 1705, 1713 and 1715, aroused strong passions and were the first occasions of bribery, illegal practice, threats and corruption, as the Ingrams sought to challenge Charles Eversfield's position. Such practices were fairly typical of elections throughout the country and Horsham was no worse than many other places. In 1715 Arthur Ingram managed to win the election, after which it was agreed that each family would hold one of the two seats. Later there were long-drawn-out negotiations for the Ingrams to buy more burgages, which Henry Ingram, 7th Viscount Irwin, completed. Charles Eversfield, having married into the Ingram family, sold out to them by 1738. The Ingrams then monopolised the political scene, holding the borough in their hands. Henry Ingram made sure of his control by making the steward and clerk of the borough one of his men. He split the burgages, by dividing up the plots and adding extra buildings or subdividing dwellings, and elected merchants from London as burgesses. By 1764, when Charles Ingram was the 9th Viscount, there were 85 burgesses. The Viscounts Irwin and Lady Frances Irwin, wife of Charles and the granddaughter-in-law of Lady Isabella, were really only interested in controlling the borough for its Parliamentary

63 *Henry was the fourth son of Arthur and Isabella. He was M.P. for Horsham from 1722-36, when he succeeded to the title. © Leeds Museum and Galleries (Temple Newsam House).*

representation and were less concerned with other affairs. They allowed the ancient courts to fall almost into disuse. The copy of the Court Baron book which covers the period 1727-87 shows that it met only infrequently.

The position of the Ingrams remained secure until the 11th Duke of Norfolk appointed T.C. Medwin as his steward in 1786. Medwin had come to Horsham in 1777 and he realised that control of the borough records could control the electoral roll and so the Court began to meet more regularly. In 1787 Medwin and the Duke were successful in appointing their own supporters to the Court Baron, and were then able to manipulate the acceptance or rejection of admission to burgages, and hence the number of qualified voters. In 1790 the Duke, who wanted

to gain control of the borough for himself from Frances Lady Irwin, mounted an unsuccessful challenge to the Irwin monopoly. This struggle for political control saw no diminution in corrupt electoral practices and both Lady Frances and the Duke exercised their political power by buying up burgages, and then splitting them to increase the votes. The right to vote became separated from the burgage, which allowed contenders to sell burgage property that they had bought but retain the actual vote. This could then be conveyed by a 'snatch paper', which was a sham deed, to a 'faggot voter', a person who was in possession of the false title deed, who would then vote as directed. The candidates who stood on behalf of the Lady Frances and the Duke were charged some £5,000 each to stand at each election. Nevertheless, aspiring men with political ambitions assiduously sought their patronage.

The fact that the Ingram family controlled the borough had certain strings attached to it – they were expected to ease the way for aspiring people who wanted commissions in the Army and positions of influence, in Horsham or elsewhere. Henry, the 7th Lord Irwin, gave Henry Smith, later the husband of Sarah Hurst the diarist, his commission in the newly formed Marines. Sarah wrote in 1755: 'He first has a Lieutenancy in a marching regiment & soon after [in] a Company of Marines, by Lord Irwin's interest'; later Irwin assisted him with his Captaincy. Previously Arthur, the 6th Lord Irwin, had made Henry Smith's father a quartermaster for the Army, because of his political support in the 1715 election, and this increased his business as a linen draper in London.

Horsham is fortunate in having a number of surviving personal letters and diaries of the period. Sarah Hurst and John Baker both wrote private diaries at different periods in the century. Sarah Hurst was a tailor's daughter who lived in 'Daniels', a house in Market Square, and her diary covers the period 1759-62. Her personal reflections on her friends and acquaintances, her relationship towards other members of her family and her longings for marriage make absorbing reading and are a unique contribution to knowledge of life in the mid-18th century. From her writing it is possible to obtain a vivid insight into what it was like to live as a young woman in a country town 250 years ago. The second diarist, the lawyer John Baker, covers the period 1771-7, when he was a tenant at Park House. In a higher social class than Sarah Hurst, his life in the town revolved around the 'top set', the Shelley, Eversfield, Wicker, Blunt and Tredcroft families, who were wealthy and provided the J.P.s. His diary therefore gives a different slant on town life.

Another important source that is highly valued is the collection of documents relating to Hills Place and the Ingram family, now deposited at the Horsham Museum, and these provide fascinating details of the running of the house and estate.

Entertaining on a grand scale was expected of the Ingrams, and their residence was used regularly as a meeting place for the county Whig gentry during their long ascendancy in the 18th century. In 1740 the Duke of Newcastle wrote to the Duke of Richmond, 'Col. Ingram invites us all to supper as usual, and we desire all our friends to be at Hills', in order to discuss the forthcoming county election. The dispensation of hospitality around election time was taken for granted by all concerned. Visitors could not fail to be impressed by the magnificent mansion. Sarah Hurst wrote in March 1760, 'Make a visit to Mrs Tailor [housekeeper] at Lord Irving [sic]. See the House which is extremely neat fitted up, some exceeding fine Prints, which I cou'd spend whole hours in admiring.'

Local people liked and respected the Ingrams, despite their rank and high connections. It was a two-way process, for the Ingrams treated their tenants considerately. Traders and craftsmen benefited, as they provided the necessary day-to-day items for running and maintaining the estate and feeding the staff, family and guests when they were in residence.

An undated begging letter written by poor widow Sarah Briggs to 'the Lady Irwin at Her House in Windsor' included the following:

> … so hope your Great Goodness will excuse my Boldness. I have had the happiness and did esteem it as such to Enjoy your prudent Conversation … I am persuaded your Ladyship hath not forgot me, for my Father, Husband and all my Relations were always for the Interest of your Good Family … but now by reason of Many Misfortunes, besides my haveing [sic] the Smallpox in my Ancient days have reduced me to poverty the which I hope your Ladyship will take in mature Consideration, and out of your unwonted bounty to send me some small token.

64 & 65   *Sarah Hurst, whose diaries are among the most important documents in the archives of Horsham Museum; and a charming drawing made on the back cover of a notebook called 'Horsham Agreements 1779' belonging to P.R. Laby, gentleman steward to the Rt Hon. Earl of Surrey.*

This tenant assumed, no doubt with good reason, that her appeal would not go unanswered.

Isabella Ingram, granddaughter of Dowager Isabella, wrote to her new sister-in-law, Frances, then Mrs Charles Ingram, on 26 September 1758:

> We have had butchers, chandlers, coopers and carpenters to dine with us, all of them as political as myself and equally wise. There is no end of the presents these good people send. Pheasants, hares, partridges, mullets, come pouring in daily … Everybody is so prodigiously civil and his Lordship is really treated en Prince and we as the Famille Royale.

For much of the century the Ingram family did little to improve Hills estate, as they used their money for other purposes. Considerable sums were spent improving the Temple Newsam residence, more money was lost in gambling and sport, and huge losses incurred by reckless invest-

ments, particularly by Rich Ingram, the second son of Arthur and Isabella Ingram. It was not until Charles, the 9th Viscount Irwin, who had married a wealthy woman, Frances Shepheard, succeeded in 1763 that financial limitations were removed and money could be spent on the place. In accordance with the prevailing fashion, Charles sought to 'improve' the land and called in the services of landscaper 'Capability' Brown. The gardener John Meredrew wrote in 1768, 'Mr Brown's men have been here some time and taken out the wall between the forecourt and the elm trees and raised the pond bay.' John Baker followed the landscaping developments with interest and observed in June 1773, 'Mr Capability Brown is there now.' From 1774-6 Georgian additions were made to the mansion.

It is not known how much of Brown's scheme was implemented but it seems that there was a remarkable transformation of the

66 *Charles was the only son of Col. the Hon. Charles Ingram and succeeded to the title in 1763, having been a Groom of the Bedchamber to George III. © Leeds Museum and Galleries (Temple Newsam House)/www.Bridgeman.co.uk.*

67 *Detail from Lancelot Brown's map of proposed alterations to Hills Place, 1768, showing the substantial lakes and waterfalls to be created over the site of an existing road. The map is initialled 'L.B.' for 'Capability Brown'.*

68 *Hills Place, 1788, by S.H. Grimm. Sir William Burrell of Knepp, in connection with a projected* History of Sussex, *employed the Swiss-born artist S.H. Grimm in the 1780s. Grimm toured Sussex, sketching churches, remains of medieval castles and abbeys, country houses and other notable buildings, leaving us a visual recording of buildings now vanished or much changed.*

grounds. Walter Cooper Dendy, a surgeon who worked in the London Children's Hospital and a writer and artist, expressed the feeling of the Horsham public when he wrote of Hills in his *Sketches in Prose*, published in 1828:

> The walks ... had been laid out with the most perfect and tasteful judgment by a pupil of the celebrated Brown, who undoubtedly found in this romantic valley ample capabilities for his art to fashion and improve ... the artful windings of the gravel walks and velvet paths, now stealing through the luxuriant shrubberies, and again opening on a verdant lawn, produced a most exquisite and deceptive variety of scenery. The translucent lake, sprinkled with a profusion of white and yellow water lilies, overhung by gigantic trees and aromatic shrubs, its green banks gemmed by scented wild flowers – the softly flowing Arun, at one time gliding between its own natural banks, and presently swelling into a more expansive sheet ... and at last, rolling down a rocky precipice beneath a rustic bridge into the deepened gulph below ... altogether formed a most beautiful and romantic picture.

The attractive parklands later found favour with Percy Bysshe Shelley, one of the country's leading poets, who was born at Field Place, Warnham in 1792. A favourite walk of his was to Hills. He came here with his first love Harriet Grove. His gothic novel *St Irvyne*, which alludes to the name Irwin, was probably inspired by this place and setting.

The wealthy Eversfields of Denne continued to play a key role in Horsham's social life despite their loss of political status after 1741. Their seat at Denne had been described by an anonymous traveller between 1722-9 as being

> situated on a Hill w'ch yield a delicious Prospect over the wild of Sussex and at the East hath a pleasant Park well stocked with fallow deer and wood and the House w'ch is Free Stone is surrounded with good Gardens and avenues and besides other good surroundings. The Hall is a spacious Room and the lobby floored with marble slabs.

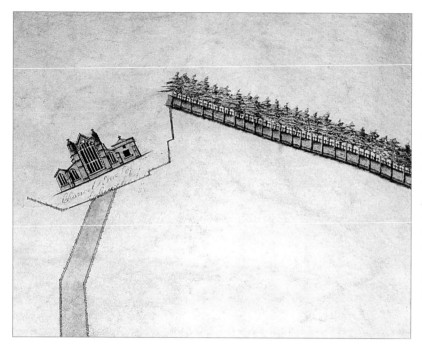

69 *Detail from a plan of the houses and land in the borough belonging to Viscount Irwin, dated 1770, showing the chancel end of the church and an avenue of lime trees that had been planted in the Causeway making it an attractive and fashionable promenade. Before 1555 the Causeway was called South Street. Seventeenth-century church terriers described it as 'a great stoney causeway leading from the Towne to the Church'.*

The Park on the top of Denne Hill was a popular recreational spot for residents, where these fine views could be admired.

Horsham was seen as an agreeable town in which to reside and from around the turn of the century some wealthy and upwardly mobile members of the smaller Sussex landed gentry chose to live here, seeking the patronage of their superiors, the Ingrams, Eversfields and Shelleys. One way in which such people expressed their status was by building impressive new houses in the latest architectural style. Well-to-do townspeople followed their example but rather than rebuild they altered the appearance of their homes, many of which were medieval or post-medieval, and spent money modernising or 'gentrifying' them; classical-style façades were imposed onto existing buildings, so covering up the wooden timbers with plaster or a skin of bricks and making them look newer than they actually were. For instance, the jettied front of the Causeway House was plastered over to hide the older timbers. The developments would have been admired, as their owners intended, by visitors to the town.

The Wickers, who were brewers that chose to make their home in Horsham, built Park House between 1690 and 1720. The house was built around an existing medieval burgage house called Cockmans and had been previously owned by the Michells of Stammerham and the Lintotts. It appears to be modelled on Uppark House near Petersfield, which had been completed in 1690. John Wicker demonstrated to the locals that he had 'arrived', and gave prestige to North Street in the process, when he completed the east side of the house. His son, John Wicker II, had political aspirations and was M.P. several times for Horsham from 1701 onwards, closely associating himself with the Ingrams. He enlarged the house in the 1720s, completing the garden front in the then current Queen Anne style. The house is mentioned in John Warburton's notes (1722-9) as 'A neat new edifice of stone sash windows in front [with] freestone Palasters etc. at ye north end of town. The seat of John Wicker Esquire.'

70 *Park House came into the possession of the Hurst family in 1799, having been sold by Edmund Smith to Robert Hurst after the death of his father, William Smith. Colonel A.R. Hurst sold it to the Urban District Council in 1928 and in 1930 the Horsham Museum was housed in the old kitchens. Horsham District Council now uses the Park House as offices, and the garden and park are used for public recreation.*

71 *By virtue of a writ ad quod damnum recently enrolled in the High Court of Chancery, dated 30 December 1702, John Wicker is entitled to trade in yarn in Horsham. Detail from the document shows an initial portrait of Queen Anne and a decorative border, which includes mythical beasts, lions and national emblems, executed in a grey wash. A Great Seal (15cm in diameter and 1.5cm in depth) is attached by a magenta and gilt cord to the document.*

72   *Springfield Park 1789, by S.H.Grimm.*

John Wicker II married into the Blunts, another family that was just beginning to make its mark on the Horsham scene, when he wed Katherine Blunt. Samuel Blunt built Springfield Park (on land originally called Dyers that lay within Marlpost) between 1752-8 as a Queen Anne-style mansion, intending to impress the townspeople and provide a suitably lavish home for his first wife, Sarah Gale, who was the daughter of a wealthy ironmaster. Several false windows were built to give symmetry, some of which were painted and some glazed. An orangery linked the house to the stables block, which was, like the house, symmetrical in design. A canal constructed in the grounds, landscaped with willows at the water's edge, must have been a status symbol at the time. John Baker wrote, '17 June 1774. Mr and Mrs Blunt and I in their boat about their water; Mr Blunt

and man Edward rowing.' The grounds were planted with many fine trees, which feature on two estate maps dated 1758 and 1800.

The Manor House in the Causeway is the only example of a Queen Anne house in Horsham. It replaced buildings described in deeds as 'le bowr and mill'. It was built on land held by the manor of Hewells in 1704 by Nathaniel Tredcroft of the Middle Temple, gentleman, who was the son of Nathaniel Tredcroft, the vicar, and had married a wealthy heiress. An avenue of trees led to the old Worthing Road and orchards and pleasure grounds enhanced the estate. The lands extended down the west side of the Causeway to the river Arun and beyond. Members of the family remained as 'squires' of Horsham until well into the next century. The family left their home in *c*.1874 when Henry Padwick acquired it, in lieu of debts, and added to the buildings.

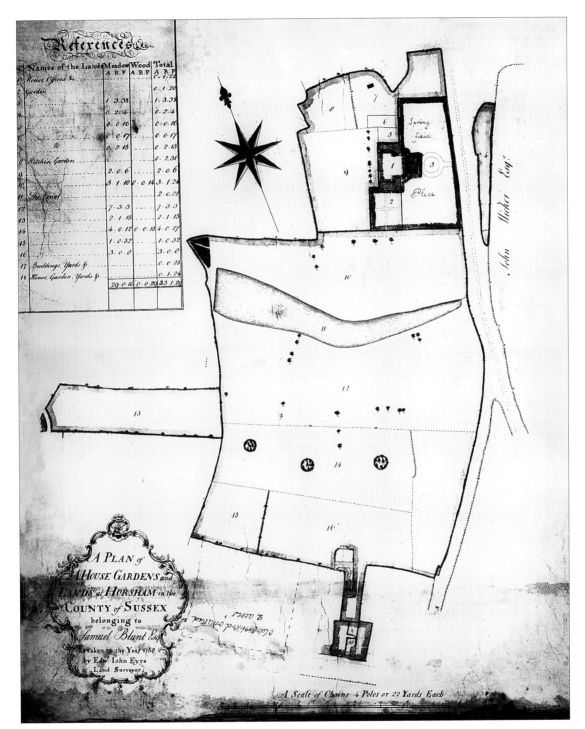

73 *The plan, dated 1758, covers 33 acres of Samuel Blunt's estate in the west centre of the parish. John Wicker's Park House estate is shown opposite Springfield Place. From the late 19th century onwards Springfield Park was a school in various hands. It has now been converted into a residential complex.*

74 *The Manor House 1789, by S.H. Grimm. The house became a school for much of the 20th century. The RSPCA took over the premises from 1973 until 2001, when it moved to Southwater. The whole site has since been redeveloped. Recent developments of the Forum and Blackhorse Way have obliterated almost all traces of earlier landscaping.*

Worship at church continued to be part of life's routine; from reading their diaries, it is clear that this was certainly the case for both Sarah Hurst and John Baker. The 1724 Diocesan Survey recorded that there was divine service at the parish church every Wednesday, Friday and holy day throughout the year and every day during Lent; there were two sermons on Sundays. The only attendance figures given were for administering the sacrament, when there were said to be around sixty communicants. An opportunity for Baptists to worship in the town was provided when a meeting house was built in Worthing Road. The land was acquired by John Dendy, apothecary, and John Geere, mercer, and was given over to trustees for the purpose of

building a chapel in 1720-1, almost thirty years after the Quakers had built their first meeting house. The building was set back from the street to avoid drawing attention because at the time it was an offence to question dogma. Apart from the parish church, it is the oldest place of worship in the town. An addition to church property was made when Nicholas Hayler gave the lease of some cottages and land to the Baptists and the orchard formed part of their burial place.

The General Baptist community began to flourish during the 18th century and became the largest dissenting group in the town. Although the religious survey of 1724 listed only 18 Anabaptist families out of a total of 730 in the parish, families coming in from the surrounding farms and villages swelled the congregation. The members of the community followed many occupations and, like the Quakers, were mostly taken from the middling ranks of society – self-employed and skilled tradesmen and craftsmen. Amongst their number were yeoman, farmer, miller, draper, mercer, cordwainer (shoemaker), fellmonger, peruke maker, tailor, weaver, blacksmith, bricklayer, carpenter, mason, maltster, butcher, apothecary and surgeon. In contrast the Quakers at this time were decreasing in number in the town. Many of those that were Quakers by 'birth', the ones that were second or third generation, did not have the same zeal and convictions that their parents or grandparents had possessed. For some the penalties that they suffered and the strict lifestyle to which they were expected to adhere proved too costly, and membership declined. In 1724 there were only 12 Quaker families in the parish, three fewer than the Presbyterians – the third significant dissenting group in Horsham.

Emily Kensett published a history of the Free Christian Church for its bicentenary in 1921 and in the book she recorded the reminiscences of elderly members of the Potter family, who were Baptists, when they lived at the Clock House, Rusper, towards the end of the 18th century:

> How when there was a big pond where Hors'am station is now, and the roads were too rough for carts to go along more than was strictly necessary … the father would mount the stout horse and the mother be seated on the pillion behind him, and these two would ride round the road; but the young folks would take a nearer cut, crossing ploughed fields every Sunday morning. The boys with their stout boots and round frocks were equal to the occasion; but the girls had to mount their 'high pattens' literally, and to wear sensible aprons to save them from spoiling their 'go to meeting' frocks as they got over the stiles. Then, as they neared the town, coarse aprons and clogs would be removed, and, the lads and lasses, rosy with their four mile walk, would take their places with their fellow worshippers; this being their weekly outing looked forward to by all, and affording a welcome break to the routine of baking, churning, darning, and general farming and domestic work, the leisure moments filled in by the whirring of the busy spinning wheel.

A study of the burial registers recorded in Emily Kensett's book, and in the parish registers, indicates that many people still failed to reach the prime of life throughout the century. Medical knowledge was beginning to improve, becoming more scientific, yet much treatment was limited to bleeding and purging. Childbirth was hazardous and early deaths from this or related causes were common. Cross-infections occurred frequently due to unhygienic medical practices and infant mortality was high. The threat of disease, that touched all families, was ever present. Smallpox continued to be a killer. Edward, 4th Viscount Irwin, is reputed to have died from this in 1714, when he was only 27 years of age. It became more common to inoculate against this as the century progressed and a local doctor, John Burry, had several books in his library relating to inoculation. People who received this, or who were suffering from infectious diseases, were sent to the Pest House in Pest House Lane, now New Street, on the Common away from the town. Unhealthy lifestyles were nevertheless practised by many in the town, an example being Henry Waller, butcher, who was presented at the assizes in 1766 for keeping 40 hogs near the public streets, and feeding them with offal, the entrails of beasts and other offensive stuffs, whereby diverse and unwholesome smells arose. He was fined 1s. It was not surprising that dysentery, typhoid, diphtheria and other diseases thrived. People were taken in by quacks who boasted they could cure anything, and various remedies were advertised in the newspapers. For instance, the *Sussex Weekly Advertiser* of 6 November 1797 promoted Dr Williams' Worm Cakes and his Nervous Cordial, both of which were sold by the Horsham chemist Thomas Mann, who had developed his own 'Elixir'.

Access to reading material such as newspapers increased during the century even though there were no public libraries at this time. The *Sussex Weekly Advertiser* was the first Sussex newspaper and this started in 1745, published in Lewes. Magazines were popular and helped widen the horizons for those who had little opportunity to travel.

An interest in books began to develop as these became more widely available. These were seen as measures of polite society – if you wished to be regarded as a person of culture then you made sure you subscribed to certain books and periodicals. There was no bookshop in the town until the 1780s; books were circulated among friends with access to publishers. Some were written in Latin or French, which would normally have been translated. Sarah Hurst was an avid reader but it was unusual for someone with her background to be interested in, or have the time for, reading and writing to any great extent.

During this century bookselling and publishing began to be a profitable business. A bookseller paid the author for the copyright of a work and then published it. Subscribers undertook to buy the book and this ensured its success. The 'eminent Bookseller in Fleet Street', Bernard Lintott of Southwater, who was the son of John Lintott of Horsham, became a successful London publisher in the 1690s and early part of the 18th century. He was the publisher of Alexander Pope and was best known for producing works of poetry and drama.

The Lintotts became key figures in the London literary scene. Bernard's son Henry continued the business and, after his death, his daughter Catherine took over. She retired from publishing a wealthy woman, having amassed a large fortune through printing government law books. She married Captain Henry Fletcher, a Director of the East India Company and an M.P., who was made a Baronet in 1782. Through this marriage Sir Henry acquired big estates

75 *Opening pages from* The What d'ye Call It: A Tragi-Comi-Pastoral Farce *by John Gay. This is taken from a book published by Bernard Lintott in 1716.*

76 *The first large-scale map of Sussex to be produced was printed for Henry Lintott of Fleet Street. It displays fine detail and is an exceptional specimen of early 18th-century cartography. Horsham is identified as a market town and is drawn in plan although the church is omitted. Wimblehurst Mill on Horsham Common, Hills Place, Chesworth, Field Place and Denne Park are all shown.*

around Horsham and held the largest single group of burgages after the Dukes of Norfolk and Viscount Irwin.

The opportunities for education in schools in Horsham were limited, especially in the first half of the century. Collyer's School was in decline and had a poor reputation. The elders of the General Baptist church founded a day school and there was a parish workhouse school in the Normandy, where in 1734 a room contained four forms (possibly benches), a table and a pair of irons grafted to the chimney. There were also some private boarding schools that existed during the second half of the century. A Sunday School was not founded until 1787. Those parents who wished to educate their children sent them to schools elsewhere. Matters improved when Richard Thornton established a boys' boarding school in 1765. It was successful and popular, with an innovative curriculum – including geography. Richard Thornton was a man with energy and imagination, and many of his ideas for promoting the school, such as advertising in the *Sussex Weekly Advertiser* and introducing differential fees by age, were copied elsewhere.

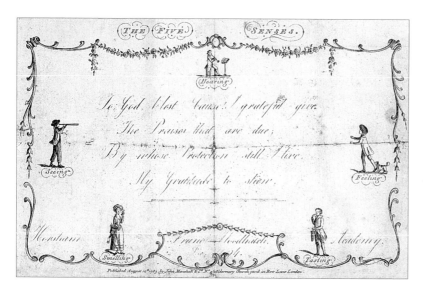

77 *A paper sheet with an illustrated frame and headed 'The Five Senses'. The handwritten verse, under the inscription 'Francis Woodhatch, December 1794, Horsham Academy', has faded but reads, 'To God, blest Cause, I grateful give The Praises that are due. By whose Protection still I live My Gratitude to show.'*

There were various ways to fill leisure time. Dances and balls in the grand homes or local inns were popular. The first Assembly Rooms were established at the *Anchor* during the 1770s. John Baker wrote, in 1771, 'to *Anchor* where *uxor* [wife] was at Assembly danced at quadrille. In all 11 couples, though 2 couples both females'. Social snobbery was a feature of the times as Sarah Hurst observed when she wrote, 'Mrs Tredcroft … says that trade people going to the Assembly at Brighthelmstone [Brighton] has spoilt it, for people of Quality don't chuse to be in company with them.'

Entertaining in the home was a regular feature of the social round. Sarah Hurst recorded that Charles Eversfield entertained 'very elegantly with fruit tea and sillibub'. One of the many entries of this kind in John Baker's diary, in March 1772, reads, 'Dined here Sir Charles Eversfield, Mrs Tredcroft and two daughters.' Playing draughts, card games like piquet, and quadrille (which was also a dance) helped to while away the hours. Pin and ball, billiards and gambling were other popular pastimes. Variety was provided by visits to productions at the Market House, where strolling players performed, and the theatre. Included amongst the plays and opera that

Sarah Hurst saw in Horsham were *Hamlet*, *Othello* and the *Beggars's Opera*.

Bowls was a popular sport – there was a bowling alley on the Common – and cricket was growing in popularity. It is widely accepted that cricket was born and nurtured in the Weald, and by the 18th century the game was becoming organised, with contests played regularly between towns and clubs and reports written up in the local press. Matches were played on Horsham Common, often on the Artillery Ground, and provided opportunities for the public to gather together – perhaps to gamble or partake of food from booths provided by enterprising innkeepers from the *Swan* or the *Castle*. The sport was patronised by the aristocracy and county gentry, who used such occasions to 'show themselves' to the public. John Baker's enthusiasm as a spectator comes through in his diary. In 1771 he recorded, '29 May. After coffee … walked near *Dog and Bacon*, saw a little cricket.' In June 1773 he observed that Lord and Lady Irwin came to a match on the Common when Horsham was playing Reigate and two months later he wrote with relish that Horsham beat Warnham boys out of sight at a contest on Broadbridge Heath.

By contrast certain 'residents' of the town – the inmates of the gaol – were denied such recreational activities. Throughout the century the gaol was in constant need of repair and conditions were desolate for them. Mrs Briggs of Horsham looked after the inmates and was paid 42s. for 'Physicke Blooding and Cures' in 1720. Local stonemasons and builders were continually repairing the building. In 1722 the well-respected stonemason, Arthur Morris of Lewes, who is my paternal great-great-great-great-great-grandfather, was contracted to repair parts of the gaol and was paid £5 for his work. A benevolent Charles Eversfield sent beef to the gaol every Thursday to supplement the meagre diet of the prisoners 'in their unhappy confine-ment'. He seems to have been kind towards all prisoners, including smugglers. Many were too poor to pay for their board and lodgings and remained in gaol as debtors, unable to be released until they had paid their fees to the gaoler. A poor box was fixed to the walls of the gaol and on fair days prisoners would lower bags on ropes from the upper wards in the hope that money would be put in. John Baker noted, '1775. 5 June. Put in the prisoners bag at the Gaol 2d.'

Crime was a major problem of the times. Transportation was now used as a means of punishment, but it was still common for a person 'to be hanged by the neck'. Between 1735-52 four smugglers, two sheep stealers, six robbers, eight horse thieves, 12 burglars and 11 murderers were hanged on Horsham Common. One notorious local crime was the murder of her husband by Ann Whale. She was accused of *petit treason*. In English law this was the murder of a husband by his wife, making her a traitoress and incurring the penalty for treason, which for a woman was burning at the stake. Ann Whale was burned to death in 1752. Her accomplice Sarah Pledge was hanged.

The last execution in England by *peine forte et dure* (strong and hard punishment) occurred in 1735 in Horsham. This was the punishment inflicted on a defendant who refused to plead and stubbornly stood mute. The person was laid down and weights placed upon the body, until he or she either entered a plea, or was pressed to death. John Weekes of Fittleworth was charged with robbery and the murder of a woman near Petworth. His execution took place, contrary to normal procedure, in public view in front of the gaol. By not making a plea, the Crown could not confiscate his goods and possessions, thus allowing his family to keep them.

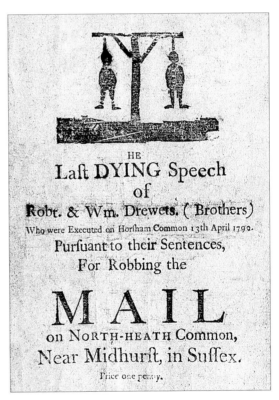

78 *Hanging Fairs, promoted by local beershop owners, celebrated public executions. These drew in thousands of sensation seekers who gained a ghoulish thrill from watching the gruesome proceedings. Robert and William Drewets were convicted of robbery and hanged on Horsham Common in 1790. Their bodies were gibbeted at the scene of the crime, North-Heath, between Midhurst and the King Edward VII Hospital.*

Horsham was closely connected with smuggling and this reached its height in the 1740s. The nearby St Leonard's Forest was a favourite haunt of well-armed and mounted gangs of smugglers, called 'owlers'. They also met in local public houses such as the *Prince of Wales* in West Street. A letter from Edward Dickenson, steward, to Lady Irwin describes the appearance of some condemned smugglers at a church service in 1749: 'The six smugglers that are to be executed in a few days, they come to church every time there is service, their melancholy looks … and the clanking of their chains make it so disagreeable that I wonder people can bear it, for they stand in the middle aisle where it is impossible to avoid looking at them.'

John Baker reported in his factual lawyer's style, '26 August 1773: Went to the jail, talked with Ambrose Cannon condemned to be hanged for being accessory as one of the smugglers to murther [murder] of Cole and Dragoon at Elweys near Arundel, in November 1757, and his wife. Ought to be hanged on Monday.'

He had a good view of events as the route for public executions passed by Park House and he witnessed the demise of Ambrose Cannon.

79 *The New Gaol, by S.H.Grimm. The two men who built the gaol were bankrupted in the process and were said to have become the first debtor prisoners.*

30 August. Afternoon between 5 and 6 the three men to be executed passed our door in a cart … I walked after to the gallows about one hundred yards north east of Champion's, the first windmill [off what is now King's Road]. Got into a Post chaise some people had there near the gallows. Mr Osgood prayed with them. At 6 I walked away over the Common just as execution beginning. 31 August. After Cannon had hung ½ an hour he and the two others were cut down, when Mr Reid, the older Dr Smith and three others of the faculty bled him and carried him to Mr Reid's and tried by blowing and other means to recover him but all ineffectual. September 2. Charles [Eversfield] sent about town to make collections for poor Cannon's wife.

Another notable crime to which John Baker's diary refers is the last burning at the stake in Sussex of husband-killer Ann Cruttenden of Brightling, in 1777. Ann Cruttenden spent two months in Horsham gaol and was convicted of *petit treason* at the summer assizes. The diary gives a good description of the proceedings: '24 June. A woman of 73 brought to jail for cutting her husband's throat, a man of 45. 8 August. A little after 12 Ann Cruttenden for the murther of her husband was carried by our gate to be hanged and burnt. She was so low and the crowd so great we could see nothing of her from our windows.'

In 1774 John Howard, the penal reformer, wrote a damning report of the conditions in the gaol after a series of escapes. He considered the place to be dark, dirty and dismal, with no fresh air and unsafe. At the instigation of the Duke of Richmond a new one was built in East Street. When completed in 1779 it was hailed as a 'model' gaol and one of the most advanced in the country. There was separate accommodation for men and women, and for criminals and debtors. It was the first gaol to have individual cells. It was reasoned that prisoners kept together easily corrupted each other, so by providing individual cells there was ample opportunity for them, in their solitude, to reflect on their misdeeds and resolve to reform. It was hoped, too, that individual cells would slow down the spread of disease that was so prevalent in the gaol. Prisoners were given regular amounts of bread every day but not liquor. Daily exercise taken in fresh air became part of a new regime that also included daily prayers in the chapel and a compulsory sermon once a week.

Frances, Lady Irwin, bought the old gaol for £620 in 1782 – a year when there were 16 debtors and seven felons in the new gaol. She resold it to Richard Thornton, who founded his Academy there, but retained the attached burgage vote for herself. John Howard was so impressed with the new gaol that he included it in his book *The State of Prisons*, published in 1792. After the gaol was built public executions took place at 'the hanging plat', at the end of what is now Sandeman Way off Brighton Road.

There is a reference to the 'hanging plat' by the poet Thomas Hood (1799-1845) in his humorous poem 'Tim Turpin – A pathetic ballad':

> The great judge took his judgment cap,
> And put it on his head,
> And sentenced Tim by law to hang,
> Till he was three times dead.

> So he was tried, and he was hung,
> (Fit punishment for such)
> On Horsham-drop, and none can say,
> It was a drop too much.

At this time Britain had no official police force. The constables, aided by watchmen, carried out everyday policing. There was so much lawlessness that groups of like-minded people arranged to help defend each other's property, defray costs of prosecution and reward informants. Thus in 1785 the Horsham Society for Prosecuting Thieves and Felons was set up. This put up posters offering rewards for the capture of offenders and had a certain amount of success. The Horsham and Storrington Society for Prosecuting Thieves was also established in 1785 and met twice a year at the *White Horse Inn*, Storrington or the

Swan Inn, Horsham. Composed of 40 people, of whom four lived in Horsham, members had to reside within 14 miles of Horsham and in the county of Sussex.

A poster belonging to this society (bought by the Horsham Museum Society in 2004 and given to the Horsham Museum) lists the rewards paid to informers and gives an idea of the value placed on people and possessions. The reward for information 'on the Conviction of any Person or Persons willfully murdering any member of the Society' was 10 guineas. Three guineas was the reward for the conviction of a person robbing a member's barns or livestock; for highway robbery, setting fire to hayricks, breaking and robbing a house, five guineas was the reward.

A report of the Horsham assizes in the *Sussex Weekly Advertiser* on 1 April 1805 focused on one incident where an offender's sentence turned out to be more lenient than had been expected:

> Edward Feist for stealing wine … was on Satur-
> day whipped at the cart's tail through the town
> of Horsham in conformity with his sentence. It
> was with great difficulty the gaoler could procure
> anyone to inflict the punishment, but it was at
> length undertaken by a decrepit old man whose
> lash certainly left no mark on the back of the
> culprit.

Feist would have regarded himself as lucky, for at that assizes 15 of the 29 prisoners sent for trial were capitally convicted and received the death penalty. Most of the crimes had been ones of theft.

The July fair was the most important of those held in the year and always brought much business to the town, but the fortunes of other markets fluctuated throughout the century. One long-standing problem was that local goods could bypass the town and go straight to London. John Wicker II acquired a royal grant for a monthly cattle market in 1705 but this fell from popularity and had lapsed by

1750 as fat beef cattle were diverted direct to the London market. It was not revived until 1790. The poultry market had always had a wide reputation. Quantities of poultry were reared in the vicinity, a speciality being the fine five-clawed Dorking breed. In 1730 John Burton wrote, 'The natives come hither to attend the assizes once a year and to the market once a week and here the Londoners purchase vast quantities of poultry.' John Ogilby made a similar observation in 1731 when he wrote, 'Here is a store of poultry.' But this market also suffered, as hagglers, who bought up poultry beforehand, undercut trade. The importance of the corn market, which reflected the agricultural region in which Horsham was situated, was also in decline by the mid-18th century, attributed partly to the poor state of the neighbouring roads. Daniel Defoe's perceptive comment that corn was cheap at the barn because it cannot be carried out and dear at the market because it cannot be carried in was especially true in Horsham's case.

Prominent tradesmen were forced to take the initiative in attempting to improve the markets, even though this was a responsibility of the borough. In 1756 a public meeting was held which resulted in 100 tradesmen binding themselves by deed to buy only commodities that had first been offered in the open market, and to prosecute offenders. The Horsham Museum holds the 'Borough of Horsham Market Deed', dated 15 November 1756, which was drawn up, signed and sealed by 80 people. This move revitalised the market for a time, at least for small commodities – including poultry. A note penned in 1765 that was kept amongst the documents of the Hills Inventory reads, 'There was no better capons to be got for money, the best being gone before Xmas day. The ten cost five and twenty shillings if I had any of my own I would have sent them.'

'Market day' thus continued as part of the normal routine for people living in the

80 *West Street has been an important shopping street in the town ever since permission was granted to hold a market in 'le Westrete' in 1449.*

area. Mrs Eliza Rowland recalled in 1878 that her father, Joshua Potter, who was born in 1764, and his grandfather used to come from Warnham to market together; little Joseph Potter played pranks on the old man, such as tipping the basket on the way home as they were crossing a stream and sending the mackerel into the water. A 10-year-old Percy Bysshe Shelley wrote to his friend Kate, who lived in Horsham, on 18 July 1803, asking her to tell the bearer of his letter to 'bring me a fairing, which is some gingerbread, sweetmeat, hunting nuts and a pocket-book'. Horsham was well known for its gingerbread, which

was sold by local bakers and in booths on fair and market days.

One problem that affected the markets and commercial expansion of the town was the state of the roads. Visitors to Horsham had always found their travel impeded by the poor quality of communications. 'The ways be soe durty and deepe as in winter that I find noe wagons will goe to London' had been a complaint in the previous century, but little had been done since to improve roads. Their condition deteriorated at the beginning of the century with the increased use of wheeled vehicles. The roads, which on three sides of Horsham

81 *John Inkpen (c.1700-56) was Horsham's pre-eminent clockmaker in the 18th century, with premises in West Street. His stepsons John and Cornelius Muzzell took over the business, which in turn was continued by two more generations of Muzzells. This Tavern Clock was made in West Street by John Muzzell between 1750-89. In 1797 a law was passed taxing clocks. After that date innkeepers and coffee houses provided easily visible public clocks with a large dial for the benefit of their customers.*

82 *An aquatint printed from an original engraving of 'The Accommodation: London to Worthing' by local doctor and artist Geoffrey Sparrow (1887-1969). It took about ten hours to complete the journey. The inside fare was £1 and outside, 11s. Snow presented difficulties for stagecoach travel. John Baker observed in January 1775 that 'the Brighton coach, which had been robbed "again" the previous Saturday by three footpads near Clapham, could not come today for the snow, which is so deep on the ground'.*

were on clay soil, became impassable in bad weather, and journeys were not undertaken lightly. The assizes tended to avoid the winter months because of the problems associated with the communications. Travel affected life at all levels and was then as much a part of general conversation as the weather is today. In 1735 Lord Irwin complained in a letter that the road between Horsham and Hills was so bad that there was no passing with a coach and pair. Dr John Burton complained in 1751 that 'not even in summer time is the wintry state of the roads got rid of for the wet sometimes splashed upwards all of a sudden to the great annoyance of travellers. Our horses could not keep on their legs but sliding and tumbling on their way.' Daniel Defoe wrote disparagingly that the roads were 'how God left them after the Flood'.

By the mid-18th century social and economic developments called for improved communications. Farmers were unable to make optimum use of their land; newcomers looking for suitable places to settle were attracted to places that were accessible to the capital and the developments on the coast, especially Brighton. If Horsham was to meet the demands of commercial and social traffic, then improved roads were essential. The responsibility for the roads still lay with the parishes rather than with the user but turnpike trusts were beginning to be set up, competing for road traffic by offering the traveller the best surfaces, easiest gradients and the most direct routes.

The first successful petition by disgruntled Horsham people was in 1755 when the road from Horsham to Epsom via Dorking was turnpiked and a tollgate put up where Wimble-hurst Road is now. Although the Common was supposedly inviolate from development of this nature, public interest took precedence. Tolls from Horsham to Dorking ranged from 1s. 6d. for coaches down to 5d. per score for droves of calves and sheep, and the turnpiking of the road

enabled the Saturday market to attract much of Dorking's corn trade.

The improvement of the roads was of great benefit to the town generally. The creation of local turnpike trusts, which were authorised to levy tolls on road users to meet the cost of remaking and maintaining the highways, proceeded so fast that by 1794 there were good roads in every direction except to Guildford. This route was turnpiked in 1809, followed by improvements to the road between Five Oaks and Lions Corner. Ease of travel meant more trade. Produce could be taken to market more quickly, so increasing the value of farmland and thus benefiting landowners. Employment was provided, as labourers were needed in construction and maintenance work, and haulers of bulky commodities like timber and chalk had an improved passage. John Thornton took advantage of the improved highways and accessibility in promoting his Academy. Advertisements for his school claimed that 'Horsham is situated on a pleasant Turnpike Road from London to Brighthelmstone, 36 miles from the former, and 20 from the latter; and is well accommodated with Stage Coaches and other Conveniences.'

Many users of the turnpike roads resented the dues they had to pay – there were 14 tollgates between Horsham and Worthing – despite the promise of improved travelling conditions, as they realised the tolls were a means of making money for the landowners and that frequently turnpikes controlled only sections of the highways. Sarah Hurst jotted in her diary on 12 October 1761, 'Miss Willes goes home, walk with her through the [Denne] Park to avoid the bar road,' meaning the tollgate at the foot of Denne Hill, where a fee had to be paid. People were adept at finding alternative routes. Purveyors objected to the tolls cutting into their profits and the townspeople grumbled that the price of food went up because of them.

But travellers must have regarded the toll charges in a more favourable light as Horsham developed into a centre for the coaching trade. The lives of people were transformed as improved conditions meant that journeys of 50-60 miles a day could be made in comparative comfort. Daily travel for freight, passengers and mail to and from the Borough (Southwark), Brighton, Worthing, Shoreham, Guildford and Oxford became possible from the town. In 1761 the housekeeper at Hills, Mrs Tailor, wrote to her mistress Isabella, Dowager Viscountess Irwin, 'Have bespoke the capons as your Ladyship desired: the first two dozen and a half I shall send by carrier the Tuesday before Xmas Day … and hope they will all prove fine and good.'

Sarah Hurst wrote that she came down from London in the stage for the first time of its travelling, on Tuesday 22 May 1759. This passenger stagecoach, which ran on Tuesdays and Saturdays, cost 6s. There had always been plenty of inns and stabling facilities in the town, the latter in greater number than anywhere in Sussex in the previous century, but now the *Swan*, the *Black Horse*, the *King's Head* (whose access was improved when a nearby cottage was pulled down in 1794), the *Nag's Head*, the *Anchor*, the *Lamb* and the *Crown* all flourished as coaching inns. There must have been much competition between the inns as they sought to catch the trade of the coaches that clattered through the town. John Baker observed in November 1772 that he saw Sir John Shelley's coach and four at the *Anchor Inn* door.

Certain events associated with the assizes used the facilities of the local inns and John Baker participated in some of these. He wrote in 1772:

> 14 July. At 11 went down to *Anchor* where collecting to go to Sessions … sat till between 3 and 4 then to dinner at *King's Head*. 10 August. NB The judges came not into town till 9 o'clock when dark. 11 August. Went with wife to church … assize sermon preached by Mr Osgood, prayers but not the communion or any singing. After to Court. A woman tried for stealing silver spoon [from] *Dog and Bacon* where she lived. Guilty. (Transported for seven years.) Grand Jury supped and dined at *Anchor*.

Elections took place in the Market Square and the local hostelries were used for electoral canvassing, with opposing factions meeting at different locations. They also provided the venue for the annual bailiffs' and constables' feasts, where food and drink were always in plentiful supply.

The inns were not just places of refreshment and entertainment, for the custom had developed of conducting business on the premises, including legal transactions, auctions of property, turnpike trust meetings and the collection of dues. T.C. Medwin, a leading lawyer in the town for over 50 years, with wide-ranging interests, used such congenial surroundings regularly to conduct his business affairs, as one entry from his day book on 1 January 1778 illustrates: 'Attend at the *Anchor* all day being Miss Butler's Rents.' William Albery obtained many of Medwin's legal papers from the solicitors firm of Cotchings and donated them to the Horsham Museum.

SIX

Values, Vices and Virtues

From 1793 until 1815 Britain was at war with France. A state of national upheaval was created as the government took precautions against the very real threat of a French invasion under the command of Napoleon Bonaparte, the brilliant general of the French Revolutionary Army.

Because of its close proximity to France, Sussex was the scene of many military preparations against an attack. There was an added fear for those living near the coast caused by the actions of French privateers, who attacked English vessels in the Channel. For instance, on 6 June 1797 the captain of the sloop *Happy Return* was shot on board his vessel; his body was later washed up on Worthing beach. In 1794 the Duke of Richmond, as Lord Lieutenant of the county, had appealed for able-bodied men to volunteer to defend their county by joining companies of yeomanry, which were to be raised by local landowners with military experience. It was four years before there was a response to this appeal in Horsham. Timothy Shelley acted as a recruiting agent and tried, unsuccessfully, to build a volunteer force.

A specialised regiment of riflemen was set up in Horsham in 1800 to train sharpshooters, taking recruits from 14 regiments. Named the 95th (Rifle) Regiment in 1803, these sharpshooters proved their worth in the Peninsular Wars and at the Battle of Waterloo in 1815.

In 1803, following fresh scares, a Horsham Company consisting of 120 men was formed, commanded by Captain Comerell of Stood Park with Timothy Shelley, Nathaniel Tredcroft and J.P. Capel of Holmbush as Lieutenants. At their first inspection on Horsham Common on 16 February 1804 they were complimented on their smart appearance but rebuked for their unsteadiness under arms. Following the inspection all dined together at the *Anchor*.

Horsham did, however, become a barracks town. It had already been a halting place for troops camping on the Common, but it became a focus for the Army when barracks were built in 1796, and a depot of arms in 1804. About seventy regiments moved in and out of the town between 1797 and 1814, staying on average three months each. The barracks were built on the estate of Nathaniel Tredcroft, near the present-day cricket ground. They were designed as temporary structures and were dismantled and removed in 1815. The depot was sold to the Board of Ordnance for £218 following the enclosure of the Common. Being a more substantial building, it was retained until after the Second World War, but it, too, has now been dismantled, and Corunna Drive, named after the battle in 1809 in north-west Spain, occupies the site.

The building of the barracks and the stationing of the regiments brought prosperity for some in the town. Many alehouses, such as the

83 *A painting by W.S. Russell of an old tollhouse in Horsham, although there is no record of which turnpike road it was on.*

Green Dragon and the *Crown*, had already been providing facilities for the passing troops, but the increased number of soldiers billeted in the town boosted trade. Landlords and tradesmen such as Philip Chasemore, butcher, benefited financially, and some lived off the proceeds for many years. Many soldiers had large amounts of money to spend. Those serving abroad accumulated savings, which were given in cash on their return; new soldiers were often persuaded to join up through cash bounties. Some had more money than they knew what to do with and there were incidents of burning, and even eating, notes. Occasionally silver watches were bought from Michael Bromley, clock smith, in West Street, and the owners would use them for other purposes for a lark when drunk – such as in games of hopscotch or for cooking in frying pans.

There was a downside to the presence of so many young men in the town: cases of murder, rape, robbery and drunkenness were reported. Draper John Browne of West Street, who was a parish constable, an overseer and guardian of the poor, and a local correspondent for the *Brighton Gazette*, complained that the presence of the barracks 'produced a state of morality bad enough to be incredible'. Words attributed to the Duke of Wellington when inspecting a new batch of troops – 'I don't know what effect these men will have on the enemy, but by God they frighten me' – could have been echoed by many residents in the town.

The sudden closure of the barracks led to a quick collapse in trade for many who had profited from the military presence, causing much distress and removing a good deal of colour and spectacle from the town.

84 *A £5 banknote drawn on Henty, Upperton & Olliver, a 19th-century bank. Horsham had a number of small banks that issued banknotes but many of them became bankrupt or went out of business as their charters expired.*

85 *A public house existed on this site from at least the 1770s; in 1772 John Smart, the landlord, died. In 1900 the Dog and Bacon was converted into these private dwellings and a new public house built on an adjacent site. The name is alleged to be a corruption of 'Dorking Beacon'.*

The domestic conditions that the soldiers experienced were not pleasant. The barracks were overcrowded and insanitary, full of lice and fleas. The 102nd Regiment, which was stationed there in December 1810, suffered

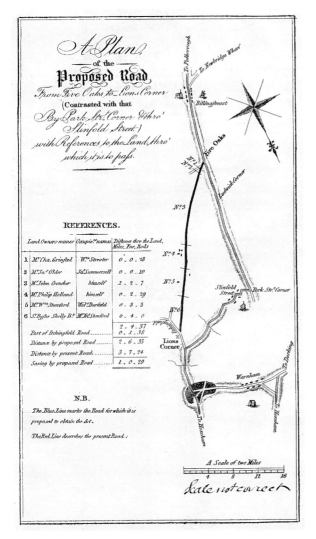

terribly from a measles epidemic, which swept through the barracks that winter. This regiment was different because it was from New South Wales. Originally known as the 100th regiment, it had been raised for the specific purpose of garrisoning the Australian colonies, as well as guarding and overseeing convicts, particularly in New South Wales. Sent back to England in 1810, many in the regiment, including women and 45 children, had no immunity to measles and died.

Private William Wheeler, of the 51st Regiment of Foot, wrote home to his family in Bath during his 19 years of service in the Army from 1809-28, and Captain Liddell Hart edited his letters in the book *The Letters of Private Wheeler* in 1951. Wheeler wrote letters from Horsham barracks in 1809-10. Extracts reveal the desperate plight of his regiment whilst stationed here. The entry for 15 October 1809 reads:

> The 12th we disembarked at Portsmouth [from the ill-fated Walcheren Expedition in Flanders] and marched for Horsham. The Regiment is in a very sickly state, the hospital is full, and two barrack rooms each holding 60 men is occupied with convalescents; a great many has died and numbers who have recovered will never be fit for service again. I am the only man ... that has escaped the Ague. Poor Corporal Shortland, who I mentioned in a former letter had shewed symptoms of madness ... has hanged himself. He was found one morning suspended by his stockings to the accoutrement rack, in the setting room. Although his toes touched the ground he was quite dead.

There were moments of light relief. On 17 February 1810 Wheeler wrote:

> The day was to be devoted to feasting and mirth; [Colonel Mainwaring] had ordered the 'fatted calf' to be killed and it was now smoking hot on the tables in the barracks, so we jogged on to the tune of 'See the conquering hero comes' [from Handel's *Judas Maccabaeus*] to eat the 'fatted calf'. We found our dinners ready and sat down to it with a good appetite, cans [mugs] of beer were going round merrily.

86 *Sir Bysshe Shelley was one of the landowners who stood to gain from this road building scheme as the proposed route between Five Oaks and Lions Corner went over four furlongs of his land. The promoters took advantage of the military presence in Horsham, stressing that the shortened route would benefit soldiers, with their baggage and stores, as they passed through the town.*

In his letter of 17 June 1810 he describes another happy occasion: 'The 4th of June being the grand jubilee or King's birthday we marched through Horsham to a gentleman's park, had a field day to amuse several ladies and gentlemen, then fired a *Feu de joi*, and marched home.'

A local hero at the Battle of Trafalgar was Captain John Pilfold (1769-1834). He was born in Horsham and joined the Royal Navy, aged 11, as midshipman. Serving with distinction in various naval battles, he rose up through the ranks to First Lieutenant and, in the absence of the Captain, was made Acting Captain of the 74-gunship *Ajax* immediately prior to the Battle of Trafalgar. HMS *Ajax* was embroiled in this great battle of 21 October 1805. In 1808 Captain Pilfold was given a gold medal and a grant of arms was awarded to him, his brother and his descendants. On his retirement from the Navy Captain Pilfold settled elsewhere in Sussex and took up sheep farming. Family links with Horsham were retained because he became an uncle to Percy Bysshe Shelley through the marriage of one of his sisters to Timothy Shelley, and his cousin married T.C. Medwin.

There were several veterans of the wars in the town that Henry Burstow, who was born in 1826, remembered:

> Every year on the anniversary of the great battle [Waterloo] June 18th, these old soldiers – about 20 or 30 of them – used to meet and march around the town. Some of them had left a leg in Belgium, and manfully stumped along with their wooden substitute. Afterwards all were treated to a good substantial dinner at one or other of the public houses … where they drank a lot more liquor than they had shed blood at the battle of Waterloo.

Local political elections in the early part of the 19th century continued to be times of considerable confusion and dispute. The borough elections of 1806 and 1807, which were contested between the political rivals Frances, Lady Irwin, who supported the Tories, and the 11th Duke of Norfolk, who sup- ported the Whigs, were characterised by the shenanigans that had been prevalent in the previous century. On both occasions there were appeals to Parliament by unsuccessful candidates. In 1807, however, Lady Frances Irwin died. Her heir was her son-in-law, the Marquis of Hereford, who took little interest in Horsham but was content to benefit financially. In 1811 he sold the Hills estate and all his burgages, with their attendant votes and common rights, to the shrewd and manipulative Duke of Norfolk for £91,475. The Duke gained both politically and financially, controlling both the borough and the two parliamentary seats. The way was open for him to press his advantage a stage further and set about enclosing the Common, thus making a profitable addition to his already extensive estates, for he was likely to receive the greatest material benefit from enclosure. He had experience of the procedure already, having enclosed land on estates he owned in East Anglia and elsewhere. His decision was in line with other powerful landowners of the times who had the influence to petition Parliament, their control over M.P.s enabling them to get the necessary Bills passed speedily through Parliament.

The Common was outside the borough but within the parish. Included within it were parts that belonged to the smaller manors of Roffey, Hawksbourne and Marlpost, but the Duke of Norfolk held the lordship of them all. It lay to the north and east of the borough, covering about a square mile of territory. An expanse of uncultivated and infertile wasteland, it was a place where people sought recreation and enjoyed a variety of sports. The St Leonard's Fair was held there in November but it was a desolate area, best avoided at night. In 1665 Richard Parsons, a local man, had been found 'dead on the Heath he loosing his waie in ye night'. Footpads often beset unwary travel- lers and the executions of prisoners gave it an unsavoury reputation.

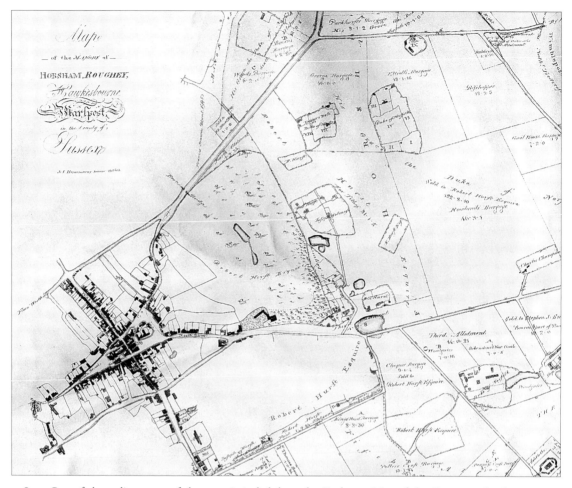

87 *One of the earliest maps of the town is included on the Enclosure Map of the Common, dated 1812-13. The complete map gives a good impression of the emptiness of the Common before enclosure.*

The ancient right of the soil belonged to the lord of the manor, but the customary rights of herbage (of pasture for cattle) and pannage (to let pigs eat acorns and beech mast) and the right to cut firewood lay with the burgesses, who had been careful to protect these for the local people. The spaces and resources of the Common were shared by all and were especially important for the poorest people, for whom they were often the only access to vital resources. Parcels of land had been fenced in legally, although the area of encroachment was small. Typical of these enclosures were

poultry farms, brickworks and tanyards – major industries of the town at that time. One such legal enclosure is found in the lease drawn up between the bailiffs and burgesses and John Higginbottom in November 1676, for the latter to make a pond:

> It hath been found that there is many times much want of water and in the summer time especially ... so that several cattle and beasts there going have been very much prejudiced. And it is conceived that the making of a pond there will be very useful and of a general good and benefit to all persons having or keeping any beasts or cattle upon the said Common.

John Higginbottom was given liberty to stock his pond with fish and take all the profits.

During the 18th century illegal encroachments for economic exploitation and for settlement became more widespread. For instance, in October 1787, at the proceedings of the Court Leet, Robert Hurst Esq. was fined 6d. for erecting poles on the waste by his stables in the Back Lane leading from East Street to Cobbetts Bridge. After 1787 efforts were made, at the instance of the bailiffs and burgesses, to control such encroachments. T.C. Medwin tried to stop illegal use of the Common but was ineffectual, despite the fines or threats of removal. One factor that probably contributed to the Duke's decision to enclose was the opportunity to free himself of this problem.

The Duke initiated the legal process of transferring land from public to private use

in a letter to Medwin, in which he wrote, 'Avoiding particulars and adhering to general terms appears to me the most advantageous and safe.' This reveals his determination to profit financially from this exercise and shows he was acting largely from self-interest. By 1812 the borough had become very weak and it was not difficult for the Duke to achieve his ends. Robert Hurst presented the Bill to Parliament on the Duke's behalf and royal assent was received on 20 March 1812. The execution of the Award of Allotment on Horsham Common was posted on the parish church door on 18 July 1813.

Three commissioners were appointed to oversee the allotment process and distribute the awards. The decision was taken that land would be allotted according to the amount of ancient burgage rent payable to the lord of the manor by each burgess, the most profitable method for

88 *The post office and excise were moved from the* Anchor *to the* King's Head *in 1733. The* King's Head *is first mentioned as an inn in 1665. It is on a burgage site, and parts of the present building date back to 1600. The Inland Revenue was based here and collected the dues from 1852-81.*

the Duke. The main beneficiaries were, first and foremost, the Duke – who used his experience in property dealings to his advantage and was able to derive a considerable income from selling off his tracts of land – Robert Hurst and Sir Henry Fletcher. The smooth passage of the Bill through Parliament was not repeated in the apportionment process. The private papers of T.C. Medwin reveal that relations between the Duke, who appeared to have acted in collusion with Robert Hurst, and Sir Henry Fletcher were far from cordial. Medwin, who was also Sir Henry Fletcher's adviser, lost his powerful position as steward to the Duke.

The cost of enclosure was met by the sale of a small part at auctions held at the *King's Head* on 22 October 1812 and 14 January 1813. Local residents – craftsmen, tradesmen and farmers – took advantage of the sales and bought up land. Some of them sold off portions of land at a later date at a profit, a typical example being Drew Ridge, who purchased three acres in the first auction for £260 and sold these for £300 in 1825.

Robert Hurst was able to purchase a great deal of Common land after enclosure, becoming Horsham's largest landowner. He was the brother of Sarah Hurst the diarist, who left him approximately £10,000 when she died in 1808, and this was almost exactly the sum he spent on land. He became a barrister, a trustee of the Sidney and Shelley estates, steward to the 11th Duke of Norfolk, and M.P. for Steyning and for Horsham. Eventually he became the Father of the House of Commons.

Immediately after enclosure most of the land was turned into large farms. There was a gradual physical transformation as fences and stakes were erected, drainage ditches dug and existing properties and roads demolished. A notable feature of the area was the demarcation of straight-edged fields and roads, such as North Parade (formerly Blunt's Causeway), King's and Depot Roads. Initial growth occurred in areas closest to the borough boundaries and along the main roads in and out of the town, but 30 years were to pass before there was any significant house building. Land speculation was led by the Duke, who built the first house on the enclosed land on a plot bounding the north side of the borough boundary. This was 'Lynwood', at the north-east corner of Rusham's Road, which had previously been a private carriage road to Springfield Park.

89 *Lynwood shortly before its demolition in 1976.*

90 *A compact development of flats occupies the site of Lynwood today, the fate of many other large houses in the town.*

William Cobbett denounced the enclosure movement as a conspiracy of the rich to rob the poor. On one of his 'rural rides' in 1823 he wrote about a journey between Crawley and Petworth:

> After quitting [the estate of Lord Erskine] you enter a forest; but a most miserable one; and this is followed by a large common, now enclosed, cut up, disfigured, spoiled, and the labourers all driven from its skirts. I have seldom travelled over eight miles so well calculated to fill the mind with painful reflections.

Yet the new farms that sprang up made more productive use of the land than in the days before enclosure, and in view of the rapid increase in population that occurred at the time it is unrealistic to suppose that the Common would have remained in its old state indefinitely. The brickmaking and tanning works, which remained after enclosure, had created a precedent for using parts of the Common for the good of the town, so it was inevitable that the land would be used to develop new residential areas when such space was required.

The whole of the Common having been converted into private freehold land, parts later had to be bought back for various public purposes: schools, the railway station, factories, churches and recreation grounds. R.H. Hurst junior gave Horsham Park to the town, and several other parcels of land on which Collyer's, the School of Art and the Cottage Hospital were built. By 1911 land that had been classified as of little value was fetching £850 an acre. The Duke built the Town Hall in 1812 – possibly as compensation to the burgesses – complaints about the draughtiness and discomfort of the old Market House making it necessary if Horsham were to keep the assizes and compete with the new County Hall built at Lewes. Allotments, given by the Duke, Mrs Bridger and Robert Hurst, were allocated to some of the poorest families. This made up in part for the loss of public rights after enclosure at a time when there was much hunger and rural distress. The Labourers' Friend Society, founded in 1837, held competitions that went some way towards encouraging the growing of food.

Cobbett was far more complimentary about Horsham than he had been about the enclosed Common. He described it as being 'a very nice, solid country town, very clean with Sussex women looking very nice in their dress and in their houses and the men and boys wearing their smock-frocks'. But this concealed its true state, for in the middle decades of the century Horsham experienced a decline and diminished in importance.

91 *North Street in 1840 was a tranquil place and quite different from the North Street of the 21st century.*

Unsettled conditions, caused by social and economic problems, created misery for many people in the aftermath of the European wars. Sailors and soldiers returning from abroad found it hard to find work and drifted around the countryside and into Horsham, unable to afford food and clothing. Some people had lost the wherewithal to graze their few animals; others suffered from loss of trade following the closure of the barracks. The poor laws of the time were unable to cope with the rising numbers of those who sought parish relief, and the influence of Cobbett, a champion of the poor, added to the unrest. The increase in unemployment, crime and debt was reflected in the increasing numbers of prisoners held in the gaol as felons and debtors.

The Corn Laws of 1815 had established trade barriers, designed to keep cheaper foreign corn out of Britain so that English farmers could get a higher price for their produce, but they were considered to be responsible for high bread prices. A rising number of poor people could not afford to buy. Henry Burstow recalled farmers refusing £40 per load of wheat, expecting the price to rise the following week, and labourers' wives were reduced to the necessity of stealing turnips from the fields at night.

The town was much affected by the numbers of agricultural labourers who lost work, for it was at the centre of a corn growing area and largely dependent on agriculture. The increasing use of machinery in agriculture was beginning to replace jobs and put people out of work. For example, ploughmen, traditionally employed as thrashers during the winter months, found increasingly that their work was being done by horse- or steam-powered thrashing machines.

Rising taxes, which had been put on many goods to try to meet the cost of the wars, high rents and rates, bad harvests and severe winters added to the problems.

Many distressed, discontented and disillusioned labourers demanded political reform and economic improvement. A Horsham branch of the labourers' union, the National Political Union, had a membership of 700. By 1830 parts of the countryside in Sussex, as elsewhere in the south east, were being scarred by rioting, arson and machine smashing as 'Swing' rioters began to protest. Some of the alleged offenders were brought to Horsham gaol, and later sentenced at the assizes. Many savage punishments were passed: some prisoners were sentenced to three or four years of hard labour, others were transported, and five men were hanged in Horsham from 1831-4 for

rick firing. Quarter Sessions records deposited at the WSRO include bills submitted by the Horsham gaoler. One such bill, dated 3 January 1831, shows that £9 12s. was charged for carrying eight convicts to Portsmouth; £36 11s. 3d. was charged for carrying 39 prisoners to Lewes assizes and bringing back 39; £5 3s. was charged for the gaoler's attendance at the Quarter Sessions at Chichester and bringing back four convicts from Petworth.

The immediate neighbourhood of Horsham did not suffer as much as other places, although there were some incidents of rick burning, but in the town itself an ugly incident occurred during the 'Mobbing Winter' of 1830-1, as it came to be called. On 18 November 1830 penurious labourers, clamouring for a daily wage of 2s. 6d. and a reduction in rents and tithes, congregated in the town. The leaders

92 *This view of the Carfax in 1932 has a seat placed in front of the stocks and whipping post. The post office is behind the tree and to the left are the brewery offices of King and Barnes. The buildings were demolished in the 1970s. The Carfax remains the focal point for the community even though it is no longer the geographical centre.*

forced people to join in by employing strong-arm tactics. Two men who did not wish to be associated with the rioters – Alfred Jeffrey, who hid in his aunt's chest at No. 13 the Causeway, and Jack Savage, who concealed himself in his chimney in his house in North Parade – successfully evaded the crowd. There was a major confrontation in the church between a mob that may have numbered a thousand and more, the vicar and the magistrates. Much anger was directed towards the chief magistrate, Robert Hurst, who received the rectorial tithes as the lay impropriator – a situation that many highly resented. Matters were resolved temporarily and a potentially inflammatory situation averted. Many of the middle classes and tradesmen of Horsham sympathised with the labourers'

plight and were reluctant to act as special constables for the purpose of repressing the rioters. Troops had to be brought in to disperse angry mobs that collected in the town.

During the 1830s and '40s the cost of living continued to escalate; many were unable to pay their rents, unemployment increased and the decline in agriculture continued, bringing no stop to the unrest. Following the Poor Law Act of 1834 some Horsham families were broken up and placed in different workhouses, either the parish workhouse in the Normandy – erected in 1725 and described as a dismal kind of place where only the mad and poor were kept – or at Warnham or Shipley. Children were sent away to be apprenticed. The new law was very unpopular with the labouring classes.

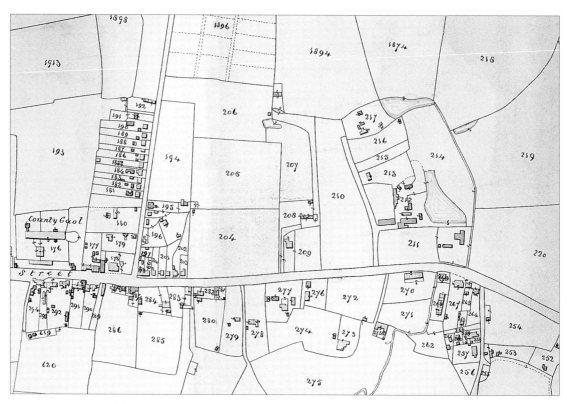

94 *This portion of the Tithe Map shows East Street and Brighton Road. According to the 1844 Schedule, 176 was the Gaol, through which site the railway was later to pass, 183 was a school, 178 the* Queen's Head Hotel, *211-17 the tanyard, and 267 a beer shop. Allotments owned by Elizabeth Bridger and occupied by the Labourers' Friend Society were on plot 1896.*

93 *East Parade was to the east of the railway bridge, at the far end of East Street. It is now part of Brighton Road. This was the scene early in the 1900s and there are few vehicles, only the occasional horse and trap.*

Richard Cobden, born near Heyshott in West Sussex, and John Bright were leaders of the Anti-Corn Law League, formed in 1838, which advocated free trade among nations and the abolition of restrictions on imported corn. The influence of these two M.P.s began to take effect in the 1840s as they sought, through political means, to alleviate the distress of labourers. In Horsham Henry Michell and William Lintott, as Free Traders, were members of the League but nominated R.H. Hurst as M.P. in the 1844 election, even though he was a protectionist in favour of keeping high the price of corn. Henry Michell's comments in his diary reflect the political tensions and public controversy that the question of repeal aroused, particularly at a local level. He wrote in 1844:

> Just about this time the agitation for the repeal of the Corn Laws began to assume a most violent character. Meetings were held all over the country to which tenant farmers were driven by notice from the landlord's agents, and the poor agricultural labourer was coaxed and persuaded to attend, and it was attempted to make them believe that dear bread was a good thing for them, upon the hypothesis that the more prosperous the Farmers were, the better it must be for the labourers … I remember a meeting being held in the Swan field in a booth. The weather was very cold. I did not attend, as I feared I might commit myself … I went into the market room afterwards and the Farmers were loudly advocating exclusive dealing in favour of course of their supporters. Cobden and Bright were denounced as the worst characters that ever existed. The repeal of the Corn Laws, they said, must subvert the monarchy and sever Church and State.

Two years later the Corn Laws were repealed, 'though not,' observed Henry Michell, 'without a struggle for its retention by all the parsons, Burrells and Gorings in the kingdom'.

After years of discontent the issue of tithes was finally addressed. The Tithe Commutation Act of 1836 stopped payment in kind and tithes were commuted for a rent charge on land, although the system remained unpopular. In

By DESIRE,

And under the Patronage of the

GENTLEMEN of HORSHAM.

THEATRE, KINGS HEAD HOTEL, HORSHAM.

On Friday Evening February 26th 1819.

Will be presented a celebrated operatic Play, called

The FOUNDLING

of the Forest.

Florian, (the Foundling,)........Mr. COPPIN	Count de Valmont,.................Mr. NORRIS
Le Clair, (his Valet)...........Mr. WILSON	Bertrand,..........................Mr. WARD
Baron Longueville,............Mr. HART	Sanguine,.........................Mr. PEARCE

Eugenia (the silent Woman)Mrs. MOORE	Geraldine,........................Miss BURRELL
Monica,......................Miss BOYLE	And Rosabel,....................Mrs. WILSON

Singing Incidental to the Piece.

"O Come Away," &c. Song - - - - - - } ROSABEL
"Tell me Soldier," Duet - - - - - - { ROSABEL and LECLAIR.
"A Landlady of France"&c. Comic Song { LECLAIR.
"The Precepts of Bacchus" &c. Duet - } ROSABEL and LECLAIR.

After which the laughable Interlude of

SYLVESTER DAGGERWOOD,

THE MAD DUNSTABLE ACTOR.

Fustian, (the Author)...........Mr. COPPIN

John,........................Mr. NORRIS | And Sylvester Daggerwood... Mr. PEARCE

In which character he will SING the

HUMOURS of a PLAYHOUSE.

And give imitations of the following Celebrated London Performers,

Messieurs KEAN, KEMBLE, MUNDEN, HARLEY, LISTON,

BLANCHARD, JONES and INCLEDON.

To conclude with the Musical Entertainment of

LOVE LAUGHS at
LOCKSMITHS.

Captain Beldare................Mr. WARD	
Risk,.........................Mr. WILSON	Solomon Lob,................Mr. PEARCE
Vigil,........................Mr. NORRIS	Totterton,..................Mr. COPPIN
	Grenadier,....Mr. HART

And Lydia,.................Mrs. WILSON.

On MONDAY Evening, the celebrated New Opera, of

GUY MANNERING,

WITH

Forty Thieves.

Being for the Benefit of Mrs. Wilson.

*Doors to be open at Six to begin at Seven o' Clock.—Boxes 3s Pit 2s, Gallery 1s. Children under
Twelve Years of age admitted at half price.—No half price to the Gallery this Evening.
Tickets to be had at the Kings Head and Anchor Taverns, and of Mr. Wilson at Mr. J. Oakes'*

95 *In 1788 an Act was passed allowing magistrates the right to grant licences for theatrical performances in Horsham. The* King's Head *was used for this performance of The* Foundling of the Forest *on 26 February 1819.*

1840 a cartographic survey of Horsham parish was undertaken on a large scale, with a second drawn up in 1844 accompanied by a Tithe Award or Apportionment listing each property and giving the owner, occupier, description of property or parcel of land and the new rent charges. Because of the size of the parish five maps were drawn. They show each field, building and garden. These were all numbered and recorded in the accompanying Award. The

Tithe Maps and Schedule, taken in conjunction with the 1841 census, the first decennial census to record in detail place of residence, date of birth and occupation of the residents, are of great value to the historian.

It is possible to obtain a detailed picture of the town from the mid-19th century onwards from other sources. The *Reminiscences of Horsham*, recalled by Henry Burstow at the age of 85, written down by William Albery and published in 1911 by the Free Christian Church in Worthing Road, provides a record of the society, folklore, customs and events of the town. Living as he did until 1916, his long life spanned a period of great social change. Burstow was born in an area of the Bishopric called the Rookeries, which may have acquired its name from the presence of rooks in the tall trees in the street, or because of its being a poor area, after the noise of the women, who were supposed to sound like rooks. The son of a clay pipe maker, he became a celebrated bell-ringer and singer. Part of his repertoire of folk songs was transcribed by R. Vaughan Williams. A collection of *Childhood Memories*, made in 1964, includes some recollections by Faith Woods, who was born in 1893. She lived near Henry Burstow, and wrote, 'I can picture him now, trotting along with some boots he had mended, still wearing his cap and his cobbler's apron.'

A visual record of the town has been left by Howard Dudley, through drawings and contemporary descriptions, in *The History & Antiquities of Horsham*, which he published in 1836 when aged, remarkably, just 16. Henry Michell's diary, or memorandum, gives an insight into the personal, business and political life of a prosperous middle-class Victorian entrepreneur. Dorothea Hurst's *Horsham: Its History & Antiquities* drew on original manuscripts, personal recollections and previously published works and was so well received by the residents of the town when it was first published in 1868 that a second edition was made in 1889. Its comments and observations on Horsham as it then was have left the readers of today with another invaluable source for contemporary life.

In 1830 the privilege of holding the assizes in the Town Hall was, according to Howard Dudley, 'selfishly abstracted from the town, by the inhabitants of Lewes' amidst considerable local controversy, leading to a diminution of the town's civic standing. The inmates of the gaol were restricted largely to debtors and the gaol began to lose its importance. The chaplain lamented the scenes he found within the building, complaining that prisoners were drinking and smoking too much and not attending chapel.

The Reform Act of 1832 saw the loss of one of Horsham's Members, although it gave renewed political life to the town by enlarging the constituency to include the whole parish. The electorate was increased to cover all those who fulfilled the property qualifications – men with property worth £10 per annum could vote – so there were celebrations, with a march around the town and some 3,000 people sitting down to a dinner of cold beef in the park. With the passing of the Act the Duke of Norfolk lost interest in the administration of the borough and the political manipulation of the Court Leet, which met for the last time in 1834, and ceased to elect the bailiffs. The borough, which had existed for over six centuries, finally died because Horsham chose not to take advantage of the Municipal Corporations Act of 1835 to revive the corporation. The Act was a result of the government's realisation that boroughs were riddled with corruption and an attempt had to be made to impose a uniform system. People in Horsham had lost interest in local government, largely because of the corrupt handling by various Dukes of Norfolk and the Ingram family, and so did nothing about the new Act.

The next decade saw one of the most infamous elections in the history of Horsham, when the 1847 campaign revealed some of the worst vices of electioneering. Both candidates, Seymour Fitzgerald and John Jervis, plied the electors with drink and 'treats', employing bribery and intimidation. Henry Michell described it as 'a long and bitter contest'. Henry Burstow claimed that 'free' liquor could be had at every public house and beer shop in the parish for several weeks and that on nomination and polling days it could almost be said the town was entirely drunk. The bribery was almost as bad as the drunkenness: many 'free and independent' citizens were bribed for their vote; others were bribed not to vote; others still were kidnapped so that they could not vote! Horsham's reputation came to the attention of the Prime Minister, Lord John Russell, who introduced a Bill 'to promote further enquiry into Bribery and Corruption alleged to prevail in the borough of Horsham'. It was not until the Ballot Act of 1872 ended the 'open' ballot that the electoral process was freed from its malpractices.

Away from politics, progress was made in other areas. Improvements in the public services came in 1835 when the Lighting and Watching Acts were adopted for the urban area of the parish thanks to pressure from some of the ratepayers, who saw the need for some form of administration to replace that of the defunct borough. This resulted in the provision of a town fire engine, with a voluntary fire brigade formed in around 1840, supported by townspeople who subscribed to it on a regular basis. This replaced the limited equipment that had dealt with fires previously – Horsham's first 'fire engine', essentially a water cart, had been presented to the town in 1740, and Lady Irwin had replaced that with another machine in 1780. A founder member of the Horsham Fire Brigade was local archaeologist and antiquarian, Thomas Honeywood (who used to give magic lantern shows that were always popular). It was not until 1882 that the first Fire Station was built in North Street. Faith Woods recalled:

Who does not remember our firemen when a call was made, cycling to all the roads where firemen lived, ringing a handbell and yelling for all he was worth, 'Fire, Fire!' And then there was a scamper, grown-ups and children would hasten to the old Fire Station to see the engines and horses dashing off even as far as Knepp Castle on one occasion.

The newly formed Horsham Gas and Coke Company built a gasworks behind Albion Terrace, north-west of the Carfax between London Road and Springfield Road. Gas was introduced in 1836 with the installation of 40 lights in the centre of the town – a great improvement on the lanthorn that John Baker's boy had used to guide his master home at night in 1770. The Lighting and Watching inspectors appointed the first paid constable in 1839 and a police station was built in Queen Street in 1846. The Denne Road cemetery was opened in 1852.

After centuries of hangings in Horsham the last execution took place at the gaol in 1844, when John Lawrence was hanged for the murder of Mr Solomon, Superintendent of Police at Brighton. By this time there was considerable revulsion against the spectacle. Mr Kenrick, the curate, prevailed upon the schoolmasters in the town to take the scholars up to Denne Park out of the way so that they should not witness the scene. Henry Burstow described the gallows erected on the west front of the gaol; they had been built in 1821 with a 'Newgate Drop', an improvement on the old horse and cart system of dispatch but a ghastly looking affair of timber and canvas, both painted black. By 1845 the gaol had closed, and when the building was pulled down the body of Lawrence was exhumed and taken temporarily to *Queen's Head* stables, where it excited the curiosity of many people who paid 2d. to see it. Subsequently he was buried in the south-west end of the churchyard, the designated spot for criminals.

96 *Local printers took advantage of the large crowds to sell cheap broadsheets on sensational convictions. Here John Roberts records the trial, conviction and execution of wife murderer William Holloway who was hanged outside Horsham gaol in December 1831.*

The demolition of the gaol was a public spectacle and 'town talk' for many a long day. Henry Michell recorded:

I obtained possession of the Gaol [for the sum of £2,560] the beginning of November and the St Leonard's Fair was held near the Queen's Head on the 17 of November and … I allowed anyone to go over it (in fact I threw it quite open to public view) and thousands of people flocked to see it.

Park Square was built on the site of the gaol, which was later cut in two by the building of the railway line through it in 1859.

SEVEN

The Victorian Age

In the first half of the 19th century Horsham was still the centre for cattle and corn dealing, and trades and professions were largely agriculturally based, geared to servicing the surrounding region. But there were enormous changes after the railway arrived. Instead of being a market centre for local products Horsham became a local centre for food and other manufactured items brought in by rail from all over the country. It developed into an important and busy rail junction with connections to London, Brighton, Portsmouth and Guildford – a factor specifically mentioned in later handbooks on the town which was said to be one of the best-connected in Sussex.

It took quite a time for a line to come to Horsham. Various projects were proposed as pressure grew to provide the town with this new mode of transport, and a prospective railway hotel was built in the 1830s opposite

97 *The locomotive 32523 at Horsham Station on 24 August 1959.*

99

98   *The locomotive is the 31866 and the occasion is the Locomotive Club of Great Britain Rail Tour on 5 December 1965.*

| M Stone | | | | HORSHAM STATION. | | | | | | |

M Stone				HORSHAM STATION.						
		162	7	7	19					
Dr. to the LONDON BRIGHTON AND SOUTH COAST RAILWAY COMPANY, for Carriage. &c.										
FROM	DESCRIPTION OF GOODS.	Weight. Tons. cwt. qrs. lbs.	Rate.	Railway Charge. £ s. d.	Collection. s. d.	Paid on. s. d.	Delivery. s. d.	Total. £ s. d.		
Wg Lewes	50 Lambs			1 5 9				1 5 9		
[W. & S. Ltd.]				Received payment for the Company CJCranlew						
NOTICE... paid, and the Company's Delivery Book or Sheet signed on Delivery; and it is requested that nothing more be paid than is stated on this Bill. For conditions of Carriage, see back hereof.										

99   *Portion of the paperwork issued for delivery of lambs to Horsham Station. Fifty lambs were transported by rail from Lewes to Horsham for Mr Stone, of Bonets Farm, Capel, Surrey. The month was July but the year is not recorded.*

Elm Grove. In the 11th year of Queen Victoria's reign, on 14 February 1848, steam travel arrived in Horsham, amidst much rejoicing by many, with the opening of a branch line from Three Bridges to the town under the ownership of the London, Brighton and South Coast Railway (hereafter LB&SCR). Horsham was a terminus from 1848 until 1859, when the next section, to Petworth, was opened. The line to Guildford came in 1865, and that to Dorking in 1867.

An unusual incident happened on the newly opened Petworth line. On 22 October 1859, just 12 days after its inauguration, locomotive 79 left the station at Petworth without an engine crew! It crashed its way through the level crossing gates at Hardham, Cray Lane and Billingshurst and travelled for nearly 17 miles until the gradient forced it to reduce speed as it approached Horsham. An engine cleaner going on duty at Horsham was able to climb aboard and stop the runaway engine, for which he received promotion to fireman and a gratuity of £3.

The railways revolutionised the way that people travelled and thought about travel as all parts of the country became accessible. Henry Michell organised one of the first school trips of the time when he arranged for all the children in the parish to visit the Great Exhibition on 24 September 1851. Altogether a group of nearly four hundred from the British, Denne, Collyer's, Boys National and Southwater schools enjoyed the day out in London on a specially hired train.

The local road services could not compete. The passenger coach, with its flamboyant and evocative associations, found it impossible to survive for long. Robert Whittle, who lived in the Causeway, was the coachman for London coach *The Star*, which left the *Swan* promptly at 7 a.m. every day, except Sundays, travelling to Holborn and arriving back at 8 p.m. Customers began to desert him for the faster and cheaper service when the London–Brighton line passing through Three Bridges was built in 1841. Once the railway arrived in Horsham the daily road carrier service to London ceased abruptly as the fares and times of travel were undercut. James Lloyd, the carrier who lived at Lloyd's yard, now the corner of Wickersham Lane, went out of business almost immediately.

The railway affected the commerce of Horsham dramatically. There were many craftsmen and tradesmen in the town who ran little businesses, making parts and products in their own workshops. Edmund Blunden described Old Horsham in his book *Shelley: A Life Story*: 'From hats to harness, people could get what they required in Horsham, for Horsham made "a great number of things".' Such skills became redundant as the nature of manufacturing changed. Unable to compete, many of these concerns closed down. It was cheaper to assemble products from parts brought into the town by rail, or to import finished products. For instance, the watch and clock making trade in the town was affected by the mass production of rough movements or parts in south Lancashire, especially around Prescot, which were then sent by rail all over the country, and in the boot-making trade the switch to using machines, or importing ready-made boots, put craftsmen out of work.

Some entrepreneurs took advantage of the opportunities created by the railways to establish new industries or expand existing ones. In 1841 William Lintott, son of John Lintott, a butcher in West Street, transformed his locally based retail grocery business, situated on the corner of South Street and Middle Street, into a wholesale business in new Carfax premises where he had offices, storerooms and stables. He built his trade up so that in time he served an area of over 400 square miles. His success made the family very prosperous in the mid-Victorian period and later and W. Albery called him 'the largest and richest tradesman in the town'. The Lintotts were politically active benefactors to the town. William Lintott, who succeeded his father

100 *William Lintott's new premises with the family home adjacent. The tall chimney that carried away the unpleasant fumes created by the tallow-chandling process can be seen. The buildings were demolished and replaced by the Sterling Buildings in 1938. Originally the firm's travellers used a pony and trap. Four-horse teams bringing merchandise from London to be distributed throughout this part of the country were replaced by large vans. In 1932 the Women's Institute weekly market started up, the first of its kind in the country, in the Horsham Market building, which was next to the Lintott home.*

William in the grocery business, played a key role in the building of the Holy Trinity Church in Rushams Road to replace the 'tin' Mission Church on Percy Road which had been opened in 1879 to serve the area around Rushams and Trafalgar Roads. In memory of William, who died on 25 August 1911 aged 79, the Lintott family gave two stained glass windows to the new church. His son, W.H. Bernard Lintott, J.P., was chairman of the Horsham Urban District Council (hereafter HUDC).

The energy and shrewd eye for business of Henry Michell, who came to live in Horsham in 1834, brought him considerable financial success. In 1853 he bought the *Richmond Arms*, which also housed the Literary Institution, the building that had formerly been the old gaol and then Thornton's Academy. In his diary he describes the extensive alterations he made to the building, which he renamed Grandford House.

Michell was a successful maltster and at a time when brewing was at its height the most prominent brewer in the town, running not only the brewery in West Street, which he first leased from the Shelley family in 1841, but buying up the Fountain Brewery in the Carfax in 1852 and many inns throughout the county. He built a new malthouse in Park Square, close to the railway, in 1860. He also developed coal and brickmaking businesses. He bought *The Plough* with some land attached at Three Bridges in 1838 and started a brickworks there.

His diary demonstrates that he fully appreciated the key part the railway played in stimulating growth of trade and business. He wrote in 1839, 'The Brighton railway was now in full operation in construction and was the cause of the sudden increase in our business, I had a great many men at work making bricks.' He seized the opportunity to sell much of the material from the gaol – iron, stone, bricks and timber – to companies constructing railway works and bridges. Over 2½ million bricks from the site were sold, and many of these were used to build the line from Three Bridges to Horsham. In 1848 he reflected that after the opening of the Horsham and Three Bridges railway the trade of the town felt an immediate benefit: 'Our trade instead of declining, as I supposed it would when the railway works were finished,

continued to increase and we were now doing more than my wildest flights of imagination led me to expect.' Over half a million bricks from his brickworks in Queen Street, in the vicinity of the former gaol, supplied the relocation of the Crystal Palace at Sydenham.

Brickmaking began to play a more significant part in the economy of the town once the railway era began. There were several brickworks in addition to Henry Michell's: the Nightingale family owned the Lambsbottom Brickworks on the east side of Hurst Road and worked the brickfield between Depot Road and Harwood Road; brickworks at Southwater and Warnham grew up along the railway line and expanded rapidly in the late 19th century as raw materials were brought in by rail and loaded wagons were dispatched daily to many parts of the United Kingdom. The bricks were in demand for building projects that included Victoria Station, municipal buildings in Worthing, Bognor and Brighton and the harbour works at Shoreham.

101 *Loading up the dray was a familiar sight about town.*

There were other brewers in Horsham who established prosperous, independent businesses. In 1850 James King established a malting business in the Bishopric and in 1870 he amalgamated with Satchell's Brewery in North Parade. The Barnes family had taken over the East Street Brewery in 1878 and in 1906 the families united to form King and Barnes Ltd, centering their operations in the Bishopric. The business survived until 2000.

The milling industry fared less well. Many small mills in Horsham declined, unable to compete with cheaper imported grain and the public demand for white flour, which was being produced by the more cost-efficient roller mills built at or near the ports. Alterations to the old Town Mill ensured its survival; William Prewett bought it in around 1890. The Prewett family, who also owned the Worthing Steam Mill, more popularly known as Prewett's Mill, ran the two mills in conjunction and expanded their business affairs as millers and corn merchants into other areas. William Prewett was described in *Kelly's Directory* of 1891 as 'Miller, Corn Merchant and Steam Thrashing Machine Proprietor, Farmer and Dairyman and Agent to the London and Lancashire Fire Insurance Office'. Prewett's Mill was the last to produce stone-ground flour in Horsham. It was taken over by Allison's in the early 1970s.

A few other millwrights branched out into allied areas, establishing engineering and agricultural works. Richard Boxall started a foundry for engineering and agricultural implement manufacturing in East Street, which was taken over by John Moon in 1864. Grist and Steele had an iron foundry on premises in London Road and Springfield Road. The site was taken over by Jackson Brothers Garage in 1884 when the partnership was dissolved. The Lintotts had run an iron founders and general engineers business in the town since the 1840s, and in 1897 the Steele and Dobson partnership sold their engineering business, foundry and

brickworks in Foundry Lane – at that time just a cart track – to the Lintott family, who went on to establish the successful firm of Lintott Engineering Ltd.

The tanning works continued to supply leather for saddlery and shoemaking in the town. William Albery worked in the saddlers shop in West Street that his grandfather had established in 1810. But with the introduction of chemical processes the local tanneries found they could not compete and the industry declined. By the end of the century there was only the one tanyard in Brighton Road, run by Gibbings, Harrison and Company. In the 18th century the owner had been Drew Michell. Later, Henry Moon, whose name is preserved in Moon's Lane, became the owner. Although trade directories described the tannery as 'extensive and old fashioned', this had always been been a good site for tanning. It was built around ponds, linked by a stream, that provided the necessary water for the steeping and washing of the hides and was outside the town so that offensive fumes were carried away from the residents – although this was no longer true once the area called New Town on the opposite side of the road was developed in the 1830s to provide houses for the tannery workers. The tannery closed down after it suffered a fire in 1912 and the site was bought by the WSCC in 1913. A large cast-iron frame of a building, which originated from Bermondsey and was open-sided and used for hanging hides, was later removed and is preserved at the Amberley Working Museum.

In the 1860s the firm of J. & S. Agate moved from Warnham and established a timber yard near the station, where the business prospered. In 1886 it dealt chiefly with oak from a radius of 12 miles, and had contracts with several railway companies, in addition to wagon, van and boat businesses. By 1902 it had expanded and was processing foreign timber and dealing in building materials generally.

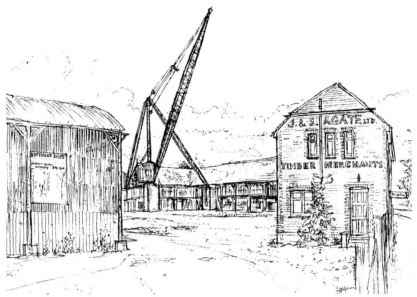

102 *The junction at the foot of the bridge over the railway line, north of the station, was called Agate's Corner. The yard was reputed to have the tallest crane in the south of England. It was replaced by an office development called Horsham Gates in the 1990s.*

By the end of the century, Horsham had experienced industrial development on a scale previously unknown. Other trades and industries had replaced the close involvement with agriculture that characterised the start of the century and building and related trades accounted for a quarter of the male workforce in the urban district in 1901.

The nature of shopping altered as people began to use the trains to shop in London and elsewhere. In order to compete for and retain customers, there was much rebuilding. Shops were modernised, their frontages and windows crammed with displays of goods, in contrast to the earlier years of the century when, according to Henry Burstow, the shops in West Street in 1830 made very little attempt to display wares in their small, ill-lit, glass-paned windows. Edmund Blunden observed that the shops were low-pitched rooms with low windows and small panes, displaying very little to buy because their owners were craftsmen working principally to order.

Many retailers became renowned for the quality of the goods they stocked. Prime exam-

ples were Hunt Brothers' Drapery at 1-3, West Street, H. Churchman, Grocery and Provision Merchant at South Street – selling wines, spirits, Egyptian cigars and fancy tobaccos – and Chart and Lawrence, Millinery and General Drapers on the corner of West Street and the Carfax – 'where quality and service came first'. The aroma of freshly baked bread lured people into Seagrave's Bakery on the corner of Bishopric and Springfield Road. The Page family moved into the town from Partridge Green and started a retail meat and food business in the Carfax, Charles Page and Son's pork pies and sausages becoming very popular.

Jury Cramp was a newcomer who took the opportunity to establish a business selling luxury goods in the town, founding a family firm that ran for three generations until his grandson, Cecil Cramp, retired in 1985. He came originally from East Grinstead and had trained as a watchmaker and goldsmith in Clerkenwell. He moved into the Market Square in 1874 and transferred to premises in West Street in 1878, naming his opticians and jewellery shop 'Clerkenwell House' when

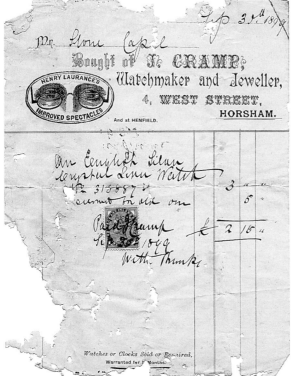

103 *West Street. From left to right, nos 1-3, Hunt Bros. drapers; 4, Jury Cramp, jewellers (with the pair of spectacles hanging at first-floor level); 5, George Apedaile, outfitter; 6, James W. Mitchell, butcher; 6a, Robert Harvey, bakers; 7, W. Kerr, pianos, stationery.*

104 *Jury Cramp's pair of spectacles featured as a trademark on billheads.*

he rebuilt it. He was active in town affairs, especially in the Methodist church and the Temperance Movement. There were numerous instances of drunken and disorderly behaviour in the town and at weekends some men spent much of their wages on drink, which made their wives irritated and anxious. In 1869 the town had two ginger beer factories, the beverage developed as a health drink by the temperance lobby.

John Wakefield established a successful family business, branches of which continue today. He too was a watchmaker, who came from Malmesbury in 1896 to work for Jury Cramp. He opened up a string of successful shops in West Street: a ladies' outfitters, a tailor's, a jewellery shop – which moved to its present location in 1936 and is run today by the third and fourth generations of the Wakefield family – and a restaurant above a baker's shop in 1911. The smell of coffee wafting into the street is still nostalgically recalled by some residents of the town. He also owned a china shop and confectioners in East Street. The four sons of John Wakefield all joined the family business. Jim Wakefield, as a lad of 15, went round on his bicycle on Thursday afternoons, which was half-closing day, to the local houses in the area to wind the clocks.

By the turn of the century West Street and Middle Street had become the principal shopping streets. They benefited from being accessible from all parts of the town.

During the Victorian period the town expanded rapidly, although it was too poor to pull down existing buildings and replace them with new ones. With the development of New Town there was an almost continuous row of houses along the Brighton Road. To the west of Horsham housing was built around the Bishopric and Springfield areas, gradually extending over the former common land north and west of Springfield Park. The area known today as 'the Common' refers to the

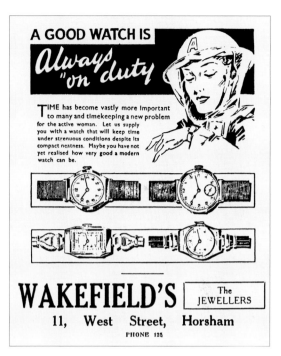

105 *Wakefield's jewellers advertising watches during the Second World War.*

development that was originally called 'the back of the Common' – an allusion to the piece of land that remained after enclosure in Trafalgar Road. (The triangular green in front of the present-day *Dog and Bacon* is all that remains today of the ancient Common.) This area developed a definite sense of identity and strong community spirit as shops, businesses, allotments, school and church became established during the later 19th and early 20th centuries.

The Carfax developed to meet the expansion in retail trades and services. Professionals such as bankers, lawyers, doctors and architects began to favour this area in the heart of the town and established premises there to cater for the needs of the growing population. Handsome and spacious new buildings, like the Westminster Bank and Lloyds Bank buildings on the corner of West Street and South Street, were erected, impressive symbols of Victorian stability and prosperity.

106 *Horsham's first postmaster was William Bourne, who was appointed in 1769 at an annual salary of £24. Prior to the introduction of the uniform penny postage in 1840 the postal rates depended on the distance travelled and the number of sheets of paper used. The system was unpopular with the poor, who could not afford it. In 1769 the single-sheet letter rate from Horsham to London was 3d., and by 1812 it was 7d.*

107 *The Girls' High School at Tanbridge House. E.M. Marchant, headmistress of the Horsham Pupil Teacher Centre and Secondary School for Girls, wrote in Horsham High School for Girls 1904-1954: 'I shall never forget my first sight of Tanbridge [in 1923] … We went in by the upper drive, and as we got round the curve I saw the house in a setting of trees and lawns and flower borders.'*

With the development of the railway the character of North Street changed. The station built at the end of North Street, on the opposite side of the line to where the present one is, affected the road, which had been considered a select place in which to live, with large houses belonging to professional residents. Industries were established in the vicinity and property developers moved in and built cheaper workmen's houses, especially for the employees of the railway companies who provided work for a considerable number of people. From the 1870s onwards more lower middle-class housing was built on land east of North Street between Brighton and Depot Roads.

Small settlements grew on the outskirts of the town, notably Star Row along the Crawley Road, named after the inn. By the end of the century Star Row had taken the name Roffey, from the hamlet to the north east, and by 1907 Littlehaven railway station was opened to serve the needs of the community. A new church, All Saints at Roffey, was built in 1878 with money donated by Gertrude Martin in memory of her husband. The Innes family, who lived at Roffey Park, was a great benefactor to the developing suburb.

In other parts of the town large villa residences were built to cater for the demands of the growing middle class. Sir Thomas Oliver, a wealthy railway contractor involved with the railway developments around Horsham and elsewhere, was one of the moneyed people who chose to live in the surroundings of the town once the railway opened. In c.1860 he came to live at Tanbridge. This was built on the site of a much earlier house that had been called Cadman's in 1427; later the tanning family of Pancras lived there. Oliver rebuilt Tanbridge in 1887 with bricks supplied by Nightingales and it was one of the first town houses to have electricity. There were other affluent families who, in the latter part of the century and beginning of the next, came to live in the Horsham area. The Hendersons

bought Sedgwick Park, where they built the present house around an older building and laid out the park and gardens. Robert Henderson was a Governor of the Bank of England. Alice Liddell, who inspired Lewis Carroll's *Alice in Wonderland*, spent part of her honeymoon there. The Scrase Dickins lived at Coolhurst, J.P. Hornung, the sugar planter, at Compton's Lea, H. Alan Scott, a businessman with New Zealand connections, owned Holbrook, and the Millais family built Compton Brow.

108 *This fine Victorian edifice was originally a water tower on the Warnham Lodge estate and was built by Sir Henry Harben, who achieved success in many walks of life and had numerous interests. He was a J.P., High Sheriff for Sussex in 1898, a governor of Christ's Hospital, president of the Prudential Mutual, a local philanthropist, and President of both the Sussex County Cricket Club and the Horsham Horticultural Society.*

109 *Dr Nowell Peach took this photograph of a barn owl perching on the water tower on the Warnham Lodge estate. He joined the North Street Surgery in 1954. Retiring in 1978 he was able to continue his lifelong hobbies of bird-watching and photography. Reproduced from* The Barn Owl In The British Isles, *by C.R. Shawyer, published by The Hawk Trust 1987.*

The mid-19th century was a period of prolific church building in the country and this was true of Horsham too. The Wesleyan Methodist Chapel, London Road, dates from 1832, and was replaced with the present building in 1882; the Rehoboth Chapel, New Street, was built in 1834 by the Particular Baptists; the Jireh Strict Baptist Chapel, Park Terrace East, was erected in 1857. The Plymouth Brethren Chapel, Denne Road, was built in 1863 at the expense of C.G. Eversfield of Denne Park. In 1865 the Duchess of Norfolk built a chapel in Springfield Road to serve the needs of the Roman Catholics; there

had always been a small number who remained in the town following the Reformation. This chapel ceased to be used by the Catholics in 1923 when the present church of St John the Evangelist was opened opposite the original chapel. It is now just off Albion Way and a new presbytery adjoins the church.

Springfield Road had formerly been known as Chapel Lane because it housed Pastor Harm's Chapel, which was built in 1814 by voluntary contributions on a site taken from Swan Meadow. This chapel was replaced with the Congregational Church in 1883, adjacent to the Roman Catholic church. As part of the redevelopment of the town, this Congregational building was replaced with a smaller chapel in 1982 (the United Reformed Church) and an office block development incorporated on the site. The Brighton Road Baptist Church was founded in 1894 to remedy the absence of a General Baptist church and the existing building dates from 1923. The Salvation Army came to the town in the 1880s and originally occupied a National School building near the junction of London and Springfield Roads before moving to their Citadel in Barttelot Road.

By the mid-19th century the parish church was in a poor state. The fabric was dilapidated and the building unstable, with pillars leaning over to the north east due to sinking foundations and the weight of the galleries. Various efforts were made to secure the building, but it was not until 1864-5 that major renovations, costing £8,000, were carried out by the architect S.S. Teulon, who enjoyed royal patronage. The high pews and galleries were removed and the great east window installed – the fourth on the site. The north porch was adapted as the principal entrance in 1884 in memory of the Revd J.F. Hodgson, vicar from 1840-83. Improvements were also made to St Mark's Church. The Revd A.H. Bridges, a former minister, added the tower and spire in 1870, in memory of his daughter, and in 1888 a new chancel was built.

The markets and fairs that had been held for so many centuries in the Carfax moved to different locations. However, they still attracted the farmers and traders who gave vitality to the business life of the town, for market day continued to be a regular fixture in everyday life. A new Wednesday Cattle Market was established in the Bishopric about 1852, at first monthly and later fortnightly. Cheap trains were run from nearby stations on market days to encourage trade. The cattle market was so popular that the weekly Saturday corn market was changed to Wednesdays to streamline business. A notice dated 9 July 1862 and signed by 109 corn merchants, millers, brewers, maltsters and farmers from Horsham and the surrounding villages announced the changeover. It was claimed that when the 'several Railways are completed, of which Horsham will be the centre, a great increase in the Markets will take place and a general extension of trade in the town'. Faith Woods recalled how as a child she 'loved to go down to see the sheep in pens; the men would barter with each other over the sale of the cattle, but market day was a grand day'. The cattle market stayed in the Bishopric until 1913 when it moved up to the old goods yard near the station in Nightingale Road. It combined with the poultry market until 1966 when competition from Croydon and improved road transport led to its closure.

In 1868 the success of the market led to changes in West Street and the corn rooms at the *Swan* and granaries at the *Black Horse* were replaced by a new Italianate Corn Exchange, Market Hall and Assembly Room, next to the *Black Horse*. This imposing building, designed by local architect Edward Burstow, was of great convenience to those having business to transact at the market and encouraged the

110   *Gardening beside the Wesleyan Church, London Road, 1905. The man on the left is holding a trug.*

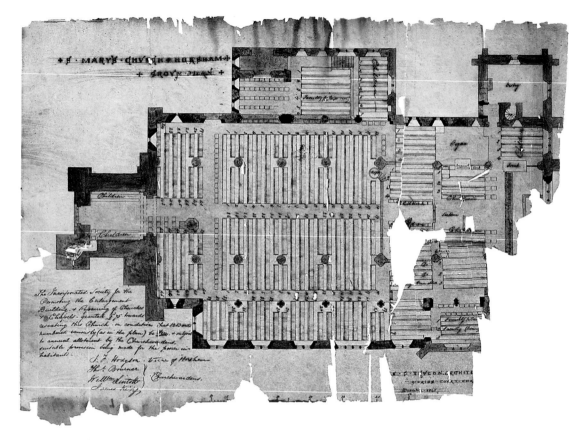

111 *This fragile document states 'The Incorporated Society for the Promoting, the Enlargement, Building and Repairing of Churches and Chapels granted £75 towards reseating the Church on condition that 12-13 seats numbered variously … be <u>Free</u> and subject to annual allotment by the Churchwardens, suitable provision being made for the poorer inhabitants.' It was common for members of the congregation to pay the church to sit in a specific pew or seat. The system of pew renting persisted in the Church of England until well into the 20th century.*

establishment of corn dealers in the town. By the end of the century there were nine corn dealers, with several in West Street. The *Swan*, and later the *Black Horse,* became the venues for the Monday poultry market in the 1880s after it had left the Carfax. The July Fair continued to be held in the Carfax until 1887. This had always been popular, and it moved to Jews Meadow, now Merryfield Drive.

Until the 19th century there was no systematic education in the town. Various establishments run by private citizens or charitable organisations, which catered mainly for children

of the well-to-do, came and went. Opportunities for education improved dramatically during the century, however, especially for the poor. Free schooling was first provided for children from 1812 with the opening of a National School in the Holy Trinity Chantry Chapel in Horsham church. The boys moved to premises on the north side of St Mark's Church in 1840 and the school became known as St Mark's School. The girls moved to a schoolroom in what is now part of the lodge at the north entrance to Denne Park, before relocating in 1862 to a building on the south side of St Mark's church

112 *The Town Hall, which was an arcaded building, used to be boarded up when the assizes used it as a courtroom. In 1888 the building was demolished, except for the front façade, and rebuilt. The royal coat of arms is flanked by the Duke of Norfolk's and the borough arms.*

113 *A good view of the Carfax looking northwards c.1912. The new Anchor Hotel, built c.1898, is indicated by the sign at the bottom right of the picture and the Freeman Hardy Willis shop has its canopy lowered. A four-horse coach is turning into East Street, which is lit at night by one of Horsham's impressive lamp-posts.*

which became St Mary's School. In around 1826 British Schools, originally founded by the Quaker Joseph Lancaster for poor children, were opened in London Road for 200 boys and 100 girls aged 7-13, although a small fee was charged. In 1820 the Free Christian Church opened a school, and in 1863 the Roman Catholics opened a junior school in Springfield Road; they later added an infants school in Trafalgar Road.

Free compulsory elementary education for all was provided by the state for the first time with the passing of the Education Act of 1870. The first school opened was East Parade School in 1873. Children left at the age of 13. Collyer's School revived during the century, thanks to the efforts of the headmaster William Pirie, but as an elementary school. It was not until 1889 that it

reverted once more to being a grammar school, although now it had fee-paying pupils, boarders and 20 foundation scholars with free places. In 1892 it moved to spacious new premises in Hurst Road.

A salient feature of this century was the poor state of public health in the town. In the mid-19th century Horsham was one of the unhealthiest towns in Britain. Many people lived in appalling, overcrowded accommodation, with poor sanitation and infected water supplies. There were numerous backyard privies or earth closets, pigs were kept for winter salting in back yards, and butchers' shops and slaughterhouses were sited in or close to the town centre. The importance of hygiene was not fully understood. It is alleged that John Lintott's butcher's shop in West Street had no rear entrance, which caused

114 *A peaceful scene in 1912 – but the Carfax was quite different during the July Fair. Thousands of people allegedly thronged in from the countryside to the booths, cheapjacks, roundabouts, shooting galleries and freak shows. 'Bough houses', which were temporary drinking houses indicated by a bush above the door, provided refreshment and crowded the roadways.*

115 *This photograph, in the possession of retired local doctor, Dr John Dew, was on the reverse of the photograph of the Horsham cricketers (illustration no.125). The identities of the people are not known but they have posed for the camera in typical Victorian fashion.*

a difficulty as far as stabling the shop's pony was concerned; John got over the problem by leading the animal through the shop and parlour to its stall round the back! Sewage fouled ditches and leaked through the soil, polluting cellars and wells that were too shallow, usually 14-24 feet deep. The Bishopric, which had once been a wealthy area but had declined and become a rougher quarter of the town by the 17th century, had an open sewer running down its south side.

There was a lack of understanding of how diseases were passed on. Surgeon Stephen Dendy, his wife and daughter died within five days of each other in October 1827 of typhus fever, which they caught after having a criminal, who had been hung in the gaol, to dissect in their cellar. Tuberculosis was prevalent; there was scarcely a family that did not have at least one consumptive member. Jane Browne, the daughter of John Browne of West Street, kept a commonplace book in which she stated that the prevalence of tuberculosis was due, in the case of women, to the fashion for wearing thin shoes, muslin dresses and leaving the shoulders bare. Others thought it was caught by dissolute

or extravagant habits. The links with poverty and overcrowded living conditions or with milk from infected cattle were not appreciated at that time.

Inadequate diets led to undernourishment and an inability to fight off germs and disease, and rickets was common. James Browne of Ditchling, grandfather of Jane Browne, noted the diet in the Horsham workhouse in his commonplace book in the 1820s. Those inmates who did not work had a monotonous fare of gruel twice daily, with meat pudding, alternating with suet pudding or soup, for lunch. No doubt portions were small and insufficient nutritionally. Those who went out to work were given a slightly more substantial diet of bread and cheese for breakfast and cold meat for dinner.

The problem was exacerbated by the rapid growth in population: from 3,240 in 1801 to 5,765 in 1841. In 1832, 1848, 1854 and 1866 there were cholera epidemics in the town and serious outbreaks of scarlet fever occurred in 1803, 1832 and 1862. The anxiety of many a parent was reflected in a letter John Browne wrote in 1847:

116 *A new hospital in Hurst Road was built by voluntary contributions in memory of those who fell in the First World War, and opened in 1923. The Cottage Hospital became part of the NHS when it was placed in the Redhill group of hospitals and was supported by general taxation. It has since been extended and reorganised.*

If you can send me by post a pair of glass containing some vaccine matter I shall be greatly obliged to you. I have a little girl 2 years old [Frances] that has not had the cow pock – and much of the matter applied by our medical man appears to be ineffectual in protecting the individual. If I get some from you I shall be sure it is good.

John Browne had already lost his first wife, who died two months after her confinement in 1832, and he did not want another death in the family if it could be avoided. In 1866 Jane wrote, 'My family had cholera. Each very ill about 2 week. None comfortable above a month ... and felt effects long time.' The family members survived this trauma but unfortunately

Frances, whose health must have been seriously weakened by the cholera, died of consumption in 1863.

Fair days, with sudden influxes of population, brought their own problems; in 1870 the church authorities complained that the gypsy encampments 'were very prejudicial to the town in a sanitary point of view'. Henry Burstow remarked that the crude sanitary arrangements of the proprietors of the shows and stalls, who stayed in the Carfax in caravans and tents, were a source of disease to the permanent residents.

The positive attitude that the townspeople had shown towards the railways was not mirrored in the area of public health, where a negative and apathetic approach prevailed. Little was done to provide modern facilities such as a mains water supply or sewage disposal. A lead was taken in 1859 by R.H. Hurst junior, who formed a Sanitary Committee. This pressure group tried to persuade the town to adopt the Public Health Act of 1848, which advocated sanitary services and provision of pure water supplies, and the Local Government Act of 1859, which gave more powers. The need was stressed for a new improved drainage system with properly constructed and ventilated sewers.

Hurst was supported in his efforts by the Literary and Scientific Institution, which produced figures showing that Horsham's annual mortality rate was on the increase, while that of many towns that had adopted the Public Health Act was decreasing. A narrow-minded reluctance to see an increase in the rates, which would implement improvements, led to hostility and opposition to any effective reform. It was not until 1865 that a Horsham Waterworks Company was formed, but this was a private company and of limited value.

The impetus to improvement came only after Dr Kelly, the Medical Officer of Health for the area which included Horsham, was appointed in 1872 and the town adopted the second Public Health Act of 1875. Despite a report in the *West Sussex Gazette* on 25 June 1874 stating, 'If

117 *The handsome Bandstand with its decorative ironwork provided a fitting place for the town bands, which continue to have a strong reputation. Carfax Bandstand concerts are performed regularly.*

the Local Government Act is adopted we shall be on the pinnacle of misfortune in a jiffy', a suitable site for sewage outfall was found, a new drainage system was laid in the town for £13,560 and the Waterworks Company was bought out at a cost of £7,000.

By the 1890s there was a marked improvement in public health. It was improved still further when a Cottage Hospital was opened in 1892, thanks largely to the efforts of a new vicar, the Revd C.J. Robinson. A surveyor to inspect the water supply was appointed, and in 1894 the Local Board of Health widened its powers and became the HUDC. They bought the Broadbridge estate for improved sewerage for £10,500.

Attempts by the town to improve its public image, particularly in the town centre, were made as a marked increase in the civic spirit developed. The Town Hall was rebuilt in 1888 after the 15th Duke of Norfolk sold the freehold to the town, a bandstand was built in 1892 by public subscription – the town had enjoyed the music of a town band since the earlier part of the century – and the Jubilee Fountain was erected in 1897. In 1902 the town obtained electricity, and the Electric Works were built in Stanley Street. St Mark's Church was the first church to have electric lights.

Horsham, situated midway between London and the coast, was promoted as 'an especially convenient centre for tourists' in 1892, 'a thriving and beautiful town; its streets and squares well laid out, and in many cases, planted with trees; its open spaces numerous'. By 1901 the population of the urban district had reached 10,781. It was a highly desirable and accessible town in which to live with its markets, good shops and professional services, improved public health facilities and rail links – the latter being responsible, more than anything else, for the rapidity with which it had developed.

EIGHT

The Challenge of the Twentieth Century

To the west of Horsham is situated one of England's great independent schools, the Religious, Royal and Ancient Foundation of Christ's Hospital. Edward VI founded the school in 1552 for poor boys and girls of London, an ethos that remains even today. Pressured to move out of London, the school relocated from the City to a 1,200-acre site which had been a dairy farm of Aylesbury Dairy Company Ltd and had come up for sale. Previously it had been the centre of the Stammerham estate, one of the major landholdings in the Horsham area. By 1902 the construction of the buildings and the successful transfer of the school was completed.

The purchase of this site has, indirectly, been a beneficial move for Horsham, for the area has

118 *In this view of the Quadrangle at Christ's Hospital the Chapel is to the right, the Science Block to the left and Big School, placed between two of the classroom blocks, is straight ahead. A statue of Edward VI surmounts a fountain in the centre. The vastness of scale is one of the first impressions on visitors to the school.*

119 *The uniform has been the school's most public and enduring feature. The boys still wear the Tudor-style blue cassock with yellow stockings, and the girls have a harmonising uniform. The girls, who had been taught at Hertford since the early 18th century, joined the boys in 1985.*

not been developed and the green fields have been retained, even though plans were afoot at the time to build up 'West Horsham'. The LB&SCR, anticipating increased revenue, agreed enthusiastically to provide a new station at the Stammerham Junction and issue cheap return tickets for visitors, and Christ's Hospital station was opened in 1902. The provision of seven platforms proved to be unnecessary. Property developers did not build up the area and the pupils were all boarders rather than day-boys. The imposing Christ's Hospital station lost most

of its former glory in 1973 when the number of platforms was reduced to two after the closure of the branch line to Guildford.

The school could have been a self-contained, closed community, having little to do with the town, but from the start links with Horsham were forged. On the day of the laying of its foundation stone in 1897 Horsham schoolchildren assembled near the station to greet Edward, Prince of Wales, enthusiastically cheering and waving flags. Longley's of Crawley employed local people to build the premises, many of the bricks having been made at Southwater. Once the school was up and running it provided work for many local families. Long service has been a feature of such employment. The Fielder family, who had worked on the Stammerham Farm before the school was built, are an example of this; three generations worked at the school until the 1990s. On icy cold winter days the boys mingled with local people skating on the frozen Warnham millpond, until this was forbidden in the 1950s following tragedies (the stream running through the pond caused hazardous conditions when the pond froze over).

120 *An 'on site' photograph of the local people employed in the building of the school. The architects were Sir Aston Webb and Ingress Bell.*

Embrocation

½ Pint Turpintine
2 raw eggs. Put in bottle
shake till it becomes, thick
cream. add graduley,
1 Pint vinagar. ½ oz Ammonia
small lump of Camphor.
bottle for use. shake well

121 *George and Agnes Jupp with Tom, Olive and Arthur taken during the First World War. Agnes worked at Christ's Hospital as a laundress, specialising in the 'goffering' (pressing pleats into a frill). Olive was in service to a master and his wife.*

122 *This liniment was applied to the skin to relieve pain and stiffness.*

Local traders, such as Prewett's the bakers, supplied provisions for the school and welcomed the business. A familiar scene on a Saturday afternoon used to be the sight of the 'bluecoat boys' cycling around the town with their long coats bundled up behind their saddles, keen to spend their pocket money in the local shops.

The school plays an important part in the cultural life of Horsham. The Christ's Hospital School Band has entertained residents regularly, playing in many key festive events in the town such as Cricket Week and May Day parades and concerts. The first conductor of the Horsham Orchestral Society, formed in 1923, was Mr Harrison Carter of Christ's Hospital, and other members of staff have, over the years, teamed up with local residents in the society. In recent years, community service has been an integral and invaluable part of the educational programme.

Links with royalty and the City of London have featured consistently throughout the school's long history. The Senior Grecian (head pupil) has, since the reign of Elizabeth I, presented an Address of Welcome to the new monarch upon his or her first entering the City. Within the foyer of the school today is a plaster frieze for the south-facing panel on the Temple Bar Monument. My great-great-grandfather, Frederick G. Nash, is seen presenting the Loyal Address to Queen Victoria on 9 November 1837. As recently as October 2003 the Queen and Prince Philip visited the school.

At the beginning of the 20th century the growing middle-class community ensured that a strong social and cultural life existed within Horsham itself. There were concerts,

123 *The school band is always a colourful sight and has a strong reputation. In the City of London it has, on many occasions, led the Lord Mayor's Show and the school procession on St Matthew's Day.*

124 *F.G. Nash, as Senior Grecian, is presenting the Loyal Address to Queen Victoria on 9 November 1837. To the right is the Revd Edward Rice, Upper Grammar master at the time.*

balls, lectures, three cinemas and a burgeoning number of clubs and societies. Faith Woods recalled, 'Our evening at the "Pictures" was none other than a Magic Lantern Show for which we paid ½d. We thought it marvellous and revelled in it every time.' A programme of entertainment held at the recreation room of the West Sussex Constabulary Head Quarters in Barttelot Road on 18 May 1906 is characteristic of Edwardian performances. Items included conjuring and sleight-of-hand, a rendition of songs, a violin solo and a short sketch entitled 'A Lesson in Pearls'. The entertainment ended with 'God save the King'. In bold print at the bottom of the programme was the instruction, 'Ladies are requested to remove their Hats', an allusion to the lavish hats with wide brims so fashionable at the time. The suffragette movement was active in Horsham, and premises at 60 West Street were opened in aid of the Cause for the Emancipation of Women, where meetings, debates and discussions were held. The First World War was the proving ground for women, and after 1918 the vote was given to those over thirty.

The example set by local men joining up to fight in earlier wars, such as the Carlist wars of 1833-9, the Crimean War of 1854-6 and Boer War of 1899-1902, was followed eagerly when the First World War broke out in 1914. No one at that time realised that this war would prove to be more shocking and destructive than any previous war in history. War was regarded as a heroic adventure, and nearly twice the national average number of young Horsham men put their duty to King and Country ahead of their families and enlisted for the services before conscription became law in 1916. Probably there were some who were under age, just boys, who eagerly joined the ranks. The 4th (Home Service) Battalion of the Royal Sussex Regiment, which had its headquarters at the Drill Hall in Park Street, was put on a war footing and men were invited to sign up for

Foreign Service. So many were keen to 'take the King's shilling' that they ran out of application forms and volunteers were sent to enlist at the local police station.

Many recruits from elsewhere passed through Horsham on their way to the Channel ports. Elementary schools were used to provide accommodation, although some soldiers camped on the streets, boiling up their dixies in the Causeway and sleeping where they could find a suitable place, such as the Olympia Skating Rink in Brighton Road and, if all else failed, under the stars. On one occasion sympathetic women handed out tea and cakes at 6.30 a.m. and the staff at Chart and Lawrence dispensed oranges to the departing troops, who were serenaded out of the town by the town band.

Horsham had its own military camp. At the end of 1914 the Royal Fusiliers (22nd

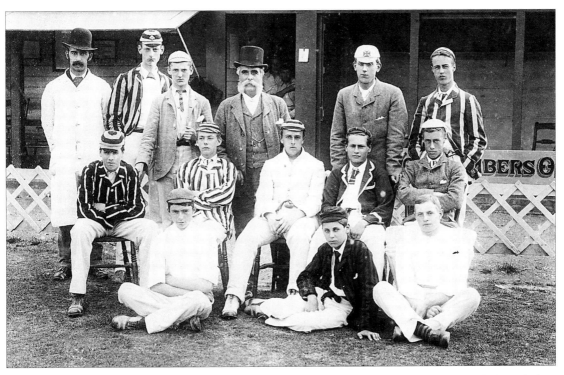

125 *Town cricket matches have been played on the current site since 1850, when Edward Tredcroft donated the land. More recently, Paul Parker, who was a pupil at Collyer's School, was often Sussex's leading batsman and also captained the team. The striped blazers were* de rigeur *when this photograph was taken.*

126 & 127 *Arthur Campbell Oddie was instrumental in starting the annual county cricket fixture in the town in 1908. This became an important event in the summer calendar with associated theatrical performances, parties, concerts, dances, teas, carnival processions and band music. 'Ranji' (Jam Sahib of Nawangar), who played for Sussex, attended the first Cricket Week, and the LB&SCR issued cheap tickets each day. Alfred Shrubb was Horsham's star runner over many distances between one and 11 miles. He became the World's Amateur Long Distance Champion and dominated long-distance running during the first decade of the 20th century.*

Battalion) encamped at Roffey Park under the command of Lieutenant Colonel Innes. Some men enlisted from the immediate locality. The presence of the Fusiliers contributed to the social life of the town and small boys followed the soldiers around, hoping for cigarette cards and sweets. After these men left in July 1915, others followed, including Portuguese troops.

Belgian nuns looked after Belgian refugees at Albert Lodge until they were recalled to their homeland in 1915. Many local people gave gifts of money, food and stores to these unfortunate people. The novelty of Belgian children arriving at Collyer's School was soon overtaken by horrific events: over 50 Old Collyerians lost their lives on the Front and they have been remembered in recent years by present-day students, who have visited the Commonwealth War Graves in France and Flanders and laid

wreaths in their memory. It has been estimated that about 450 people connected in some way with Horsham died on active service or as a result of wounds sustained; that was nearly one in four men of serviceable age. The Holy Trinity Chapel in the parish church contains memorials to the dead of both world wars and the Colours of the 4th Battalion of the Royal Sussex Regiment.

Although it was generally thought the war would be over by Christmas 1914, events dictated otherwise. Caught up in the surge of national pride, many residents rose to the challenges of the time through an involvement with civilian work. The Red Cross was active in the town and there were appeals for various relief funds and special money-raising efforts. Some of those who hunted in the neighbourhood supplied horses that were used in France.

128 *Looking westward along East Street at soldiers leaving Horsham on their way to the 'European War', 10 September 1914.*

129 *Football matches played an important part in the town following the founding of the first Horsham Football Club in 1871, although its existence in the early days depended upon enough players being available to form a side. Most of the young men would have left for the war when the match advertised on this poster took place in 1915.*

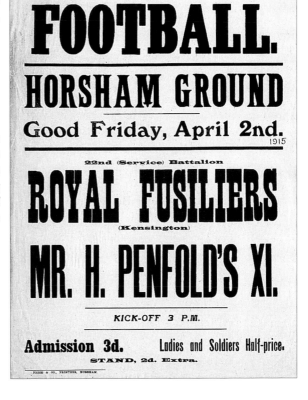

130 *A group of Collyer's students pays homage to Old Collyerians.*

131 *This wreath was laid for those Collyer's men whose bodies were never recovered after the Somme battle in 1916.*

COLLYER'S COLLEGE

HONOR DEO
1532

HORSHAM, WEST SUSSEX

In memory of our fallen brothers commemorated on the Thiepval Memorial who died in the service of their country at the Somme and have no known graves:

JOHN ARTHUR ROPE Second Lieutenant, The Queen's (Royal West Surrey Regt.) who died on Thursday, 24th August 1916. Age 25.

ALFRED GREENFIELD of 42, Barrington Rd., Horsham, Serjeant, London Regt (Prince of Wales' Own Civil Service Rifles) who died on Friday, 15th September 1916. Age 21.

ROBERT ADAMS Lance Corporal, The Queen's (Royal West Surrey Regt.) who died on Saturday, 15th July 1916

MAURICE BOTTING of Hill Side, Loswood, Billingshurst, Private, London Regt (Prince of Wales' Own Civil Service Rifles) who died on Friday, 15th September 1916. Age 21.

SIDNEY WAKER STEWART, Private, 13th Bn. Royal Sussex Regt, who died on Friday, 27th October, 1917. Age 27.

this wreath was placed by students of the College of Richard Collyer, November 2003

132 *Citation attached to the wreath.*

Hilaire Belloc, thinker, writer, historian, politician and lecturer, who was living at King's Land, Shipley, was active in the war effort. His father was of Basque origin and he held a lifelong hostility towards the Germans. His positive support for the war was seen at a local level in various ways. In January 1915 the plight of the Belgians was brought to the attention of Horsham people when he lectured on 'The Strategy of the War' for the Belgian Relief Fund, organised by the Horsham Literary and Debating Society. In 1917 he lent French war films to the Carfax Theatre in aid of the Horsham War Supply Depot. In May 1918 he was one of the speakers at a public meeting in the Town Hall that discussed the food position. Three months later Belloc's eldest son, Louis, was killed whilst serving as a pilot in the Royal Flying Corps, aged 20. His youngest son was to die in the Second World War.

Rationing of food and other restrictions affected everyone in the town. Lectures showing how to make the most of cheap food were given, such as the lantern lecture at the Friends' Meeting House in December 1915 called 'Cheapest and Best Foods'. The HUDC encouraged people to apply for allotments and made supplies of seed potatoes available at cost price.

Public notices with regulations regarding household fuel and lighting were displayed, and shops closed early to further restrict consumption. The Acting Chief Constable of West Sussex, Horace Ellis, issued a notice from the Chief Constable's Office in Horsham in September 1915, warning people of the dangers of lights from vehicles.

Businesses, schools and industries coped as best they could with restrictions, depleted work forces and personal tragedies. Appeals went out for skilled workmen to enroll for war work at

133 *Two old Collyerians are buried at Arras Cemetery; there is also a memorial to a missing Collyerian.*

134 *Jury Cramp is seated holding his grandson Cecil.*

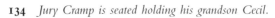

the Munitions Work Bureau at 23 Queen Street and for volunteers to maintain essential services. Various war stores were established in the town. Ammunition and small arms manufacturers employed local women. Prewett's Mill had a small factory. Two of the local doctors, Dr Reginald Jamieson and Dr Arthur Sturdy, both served in the forces. Dr Sturdy never returned, dying from dysentery in Bombay. Dr Edward Bostock, who gave a speech of welcome to the returning 4th Sussex in 1919 at a civic reception, lost three sons in the war. After the war two new doctors joined the North Street practice – Geoffrey Sparrow and Westcott Dew – both of whom had been awarded the Military Cross.

One way of keeping up morale was through entertainment. This was not restricted during the war. Dances and concerts were popular and, additionally, often raised money for different causes, such as the 4th Royal Sussex Regiment, the Horsham War Depot and various national relief efforts. Venues included the *King's Head*, Assembly Rooms and the Albion Hall. The Horsham Borough Silver Band gave many performances, even though the playing membership was reduced from 28 to nine, as members joined the services. It continued performing throughout the war, determined not to be beaten by adverse events.

The War Hospital Supply Depot at No. 8 Causeway was an extremely effective organisation established to alleviate the suffering of the sick and wounded by procuring materials for hospital use, making them up in the correct way

135 *This memorial was erected in 1920 and unveiled on Armistice Day in 1921, although this picture is of a later date. The original structure was moved by the HDC to its present location on the north side of the Carfax in 1992, when the names of casualties of the Second World War were added.*

136 *'In honour of the patriotic women of the Horsham War Hospital Supply Depot who worked in this house during the Great War 1914-18.'*

137 *The architect of the Capitol Theatre was L.H. Parsons of Goodman and Kay.*

and sending them to places where they were most urgently required. Consignments including splints, head and roller bandages, pneumonia jackets, sterilised swabs and dressings were sent weekly to dressing stations and hospitals in France, Italy, Malta and Salonica. Regular reports in the paper gave the names of those who had donated gifts, either of money or in kind, and appeals for items ranging from Singer sewing machines to old pieces of linoleum to make up slippers were made. Many willing workers gave up their time to come and help at the centre. Four months after the depot was opened in July 1915 there were 870 on the roll, and during one week in November 2,848 articles were dispatched abroad. The class distinctions of the day were highlighted through regular reports in the *West Sussex County Times* (hereafter *WSCT*), which named those ladies who gave up their time to make the tea for the workers.

In 1918 125 German prisoners were held in Horsham and worked on the land. They were

kept in a disused brewery premises near the corner of the Bishopric and Worthing Road. But in November of that year the country finally emerged from one of the most turbulent periods in its history and the people of Horsham, as elsewhere, strove to return to normality. A successful move was the building of the Capitol Theatre in 1923. Employment was given to ex-servicemen, especially bandsmen of the 4th Battalion, who provided the music for the silent films of the period. This was thanks to the inspiration of Major R.C.G. Middleton, M.C., who set up the Blue Flash Association for demobilised men from the Royal Sussex Regiment. It was possibly so called because of the blue shoulder flash worn as part of the regimental uniform.

In 1926 Councillor Nellie Laughton laid out the Garden of Remembrance, beside the river Arun between the parish church and the cricket ground. She developed the garden so that it included a playground and lido. She was quoted in the *Sussex Daily News,* some years later in 1937 saying:

> My idea was that the children should have somewhere safe and congenial in which to play. When this Garden was opened they only had their little back yards and the roads for their children's games; but in the Garden they can paddle, sail their boats and play to their hearts content.

It is perhaps not unsurprising that 'Lady Bountiful', as she was called, is still remembered with affection by those who were children at the time, not least because she used to give out threepenny bits as a little extra pocket money. In 1934 unemployed people were used to build the open-air swimming pool in Horsham Park and this proved to be another valued civic amenity; on one hot weekend in July 1935 2,162 bathers used the pool. The creation of jobs was actively encouraged by the HUDC through the construction of an industrial zone north of the railway line and

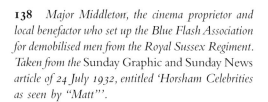

138 *Major Middleton, the cinema proprietor and local benefactor who set up the Blue Flash Association for demobilised men from the Royal Sussex Regiment. Taken from the* Sunday Graphic and Sunday News *article of 24 July 1932, entitled 'Horsham Celebrities as seen by "Matt"'.*

south of Parsonage Road. The arrival of the headquarters of the pharmaceutical company CIBA in 1937 was an important step in the growth of light industry, and the novelty of a 'factory' in the town was quite a talking point at the time.

During the 1920s the population grew steadily, reaching 13,580 in 1931. Horsham became a popular residential town for the wealthy and middle classes. Shorter working hours, better transport and available building land enabled an increasing number of people to live in the town, away from their place of work. Many moved out from London, and this resulted in developments on the outskirts of the town, including the former Common area and Worthing Road after the land was sold in 1925. Residential developments in the 1920s on Hills Place land recall the family associations in the names of new roads – Middleton Road, Ingram Close and Irwin Drive. It was at this time that Hills

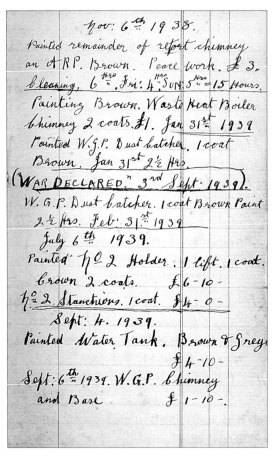

139 *A page of Ronald Hendrie's workbook covering the period when war broke out.*

rail service was matched by improvements in the roads and the growth of car ownership encouraged more people to live here.

The expanding population put pressure on the educational resources in the town. Primary educational needs were provided through 11 council schools for children aged five to thirteen. Whilst provision was made at Collyer's for boys of secondary school age, similar resources for girls were very limited. The Pupil Teacher Centre had opened in 1904 in the Sunday School rooms of the Methodist Chapel in inadequate and cramped premises, 'mid gaswork's fumes and piglets squeals', in the words of retired teacher Miss Dorothy Leslie, referring to the constant noise from the shovelling of coke in the gas works nearby and from the organ in the chapel that was often in use. However, in 1924 the WSCC bought Tanbridge House and this became the Girls' High School.

An unusual document in the possession of a Horsham-born resident gives a detailed account of the problems encountered by a young man trying to work in and around Horsham during the difficult years of depression and unemployment in the 1920s and '30s and disillusioned by 'a country fit for heroes'. Ronald Hendrie, son of Scottish parents who had come down south looking for work, left Warnham school aged 14 in August 1919. He wrote down in a 'workbook' all his employment from the time he left school until 1955. He was frequently out of work and always on the look out for more, preferably outdoors. His first job, which lasted 19 months, was working as an errand boy for F. Branch, baker and grocer in Warnham. He then had a series of casual jobs, which included working at the brickyards in Warnham, as a labourer at Lintott Engineering Works and as a goods yard porter at Horsham station.

A page from his workbook gives a clear picture of the type of jobs he undertook working for the WSCC in 1926:

Barn was converted into a house. This may have been an older building that had served as stables for the 'big house' or it may have been built from reused materials from Hills Place. It is now Bishop's House, the residence of the Bishop of Horsham. Hills Farm was sold for redevelopment in 1972, and more homes were built in the 1980s after the last of the land had been sold.

Horsham changed from a market town into a dormitory town with an increase in commuters to London attracted by the 'Workers Tickets' that were cheaper if purchased before 7 a.m. After the railway line was electrified in 1938 more commuters arrived. The improved

One day brought 'Penfolds', Steam Roller, to Southwater from Petworth 18 miles. 6 weeks dragging chain for Surveyor who was making Ordnance Survey Map of the Horsham to Brighton Road from Round House Corner to Mannings Heath. 6 months in Carpenter's shop, 3 months with Blacksmith. Road tarring. Grass cutting with sickle, 2 months. Concrete curb making. Tar Mac making by hand, and by machine. Mate on Claton and Shuttleworth Steam Waggon. Steam Roller. Steam Traction Engine, and Mate on 3 ton Denis Motor Lorry. Finished on Nov. 5th 1926.

Although he had married Olive Jupp in 1925 he took the opportunity to sail to New Zealand on the passenger liner SS *Athenic* as a foreman on 9 November 1926. The ship was sold to a Norwegian company in 1927, so on 12 March 1927, after docking back in London, Ronald was out of work again and forced to return to Horsham to look for another job. It was 14 years before he gained a permanent job – working for the Horsham Gas Company Ltd, by which time he was a family man and living on 'The Common'.

There are a few significant entries included in the notes, both of a personal and general nature, such as the comments: 'Dec. 1st 1933 Started Coal gas stoking permanent'; 'Fractured Radius (at elbow) injured chest and shoulder. Fell from No 2 holder tank wall Nov. 5th 1941'; '"WAR DECLARED" Sept. 3rd 1939'; 'Japan declared War on Britain and the U.S. Dec. 8th 1941'. The gas company would not release him for recruitment so he continued at the gas works for the duration of the war, finally being made redundant on 4 June 1955 when the works were shut down.

The reality of another world war became increasingly evident as the 1930s progressed. The rise of fascism in the country affected Horsham, for the British Union of Fascists maintained a local branch in Denne Road, and the 'Blackshirts' were seen about the town. On one occasion Sir Oswald Mosley addressed a meeting in the Drill Hall in Denne Road. A branch of the Mosley family lived at Mannings Heath, but they had little to do with any political activity.

After war broke out in 1939 the town made preparations in case of a land attack by the Germans. Two anti-aircraft guns were installed on runners inside the Drill Hall. Pillboxes along the river, tank traps known as 'dragons' teeth' (the remains of which can still be seen in the Causeway) and barbed wire entanglements

140 *Driver Scrace and fireman Manville on board the 32521 at Horsham station on 18 April 1953.*

covering large stretches of the town were put in place. There were wooden piles in the river, which was deepened and widened, and concrete roadblocks. The Observer Corps headquarters behind the Drill Hall played a vital role during the war. It covered a significant portion of Sussex and was in the forefront of Britain's defence. Renamed the Royal Observer Corps (hereafter ROC) in April 1941, it later became part of the Royal Air Force. Manned 24 hours a day, it relayed details of incoming aircraft from outlying ROC outposts to RAF Fighter Command. Full-time women members of the Corps plotted the movements of enemy aircraft, VI rockets and doodlebugs on a giant map. The ROC became a social club, to the dislike of some in the town, and it was booed in the Victory Parade through the Carfax. In those days class distinctions were still clear-cut, the 'professions v. trade' divide generating much ill feeling.

All young men aged 17-35 had to enlist unless exempt like Ronald Hendrie, and all the territorial soldiers became regulars. Many women did heavy or skilled work normally done by the men. Most people who remained were involved in some form of civil defence work, such as fire-watching. A pipeline from the river to the Carfax kept a 10,000-gallon tank supplied with water. Horsham Fire Brigade became a unit of the National Fire Service, and firemen attended most of the wartime incidents in and around the town. Ambulance drivers slept in the Ritz Cinema so as to be near the garage if needed in an emergency. Able-bodied men took their turns on air-raid patrol, with the St John's Ambulance Station in Park Street and No. 8 Causeway acting as ARP control centres. A watchful eye was kept on blackouts for air raids were frequent as German bombers aiming for London flew overhead. The *King's Arms* was the headquarters of the Home Guard, who had three vital local areas to guard, the reservoirs on Forest Road and Magpie Lane and the Observer Corps headquarters.

141 *Five women were employed in Jim Wakefield's factory, but after October 1945 the numbers were reduced to two and by 1948 the factory had closed.*

142 *The kindergarten classes join together for a concert in 1938. The disastrous fire that destroyed the school on 12 January 1940 did not destroy the loyalties of the pupils. Reunions took place in 1984 and 1985.*

A prime example of the volunteer workers' contribution to the war effort was the formation of the Patriot Engineers, a group of around 240 volunteers who were prepared to give up their leisure hours to work at repetitive tasks in a factory. The project was the inspiration of Mr Thomas Greenhough, engineer, following an appeal by Sir Stafford Cripps, the Ambassador to Russia, for increased production of munitions. Between 1942–5, and sponsored by the local Rotary Club, a small factory was set up in a converted motor car showroom given by Rice Brothers. Munitions and components for a radio life-saving device and for aeroplanes for the Ministry of Aircraft Production were finally produced. The scheme aroused local, national and international interest

and public recognition was won when Sir Stafford, by then Minister for Aircraft Production, and Lady Cripps visited the Patriots at their factory in October 1944 and accepted a cheque for £3,000.

Local industries were inevitably involved in wartime production. In 1939 Lintotts Engineering Ltd turned to munitions work, which led to a close relationship with the Ministry of Defence, especially the Admiralty. Brickmaking works, such as those in Southwater and Warnham, worked 24 hours a day. The Arun Engineering Company supplied the 'Arun' sawbench to the government. Jim Wakefield, the jeweller in West Street, set up a small factory at the back of his premises and six employees made components for Spitfires.

143 *The age of steam. The down train replenishing water tanks at Horsham station, 15 July 1960.*

The CIBA factory was also caught up in wartime work; Mrs Sylvia Standing has provided a vignette of her experiences. She recalled:

I started work at 14 at CIBA, and sometimes worked until 8 p.m. from 8.30 a.m. when urgent medical supplies were being made for export to Russia. We also worked on Saturday mornings. CIBA was a prime target for bombers, and there was a raid aimed at the building, but the stick of bombs fell short ... We had a large shelter in the basement, but when the V1s came there wasn't time to go there, so we had to take cover behind machinery, where we became expert at noughts and crosses. When a flying bomb came over we then hung out of the windows to see where it was going ... The contrast between the roar of its engine and the silence when it cut out before crashing was unnerving, and that was the time to dive for cover. If I see one on a film, I still feel the urge to throw myself down.

The memories of other residents who lived through 1939-45 have been collated in recent years and these provide valuable insights into the impact of the war at a local level and the ways in which people rose to the challenge. The Sunday morning of 3 September 1939, when Neville Chamberlain announced that 'We are therefore at war with Germany', made a lasting impression. Even today people can remember the sirens wailing in the town almost immediately after the declaration, where they were and what they were doing.

Brick air-raid shelters in the streets, Andover and Morrison shelters, criss-crossed tape on windows, gas masks, identity cards and discs all featured in wartime Horsham. Registering with a grocer, milkman and butcher, and rationing of food, clothes and other necessities were obligatory and an integral part of everyday life. Urged to 'Dig for Victory', gardens were turned over to production; some people kept livestock to supplement their food intake and every type of fruit was picked for jam making. St Mark's Church was used as a food store. A degree of inter-dependence developed as the war continued, and people have said that the community spirit they experienced during those years is less evident today. Firemen supported their hard-pressed colleagues in London, Portsmouth and Southampton during air raids. Alicia Hemming, *née* Lintott, stationed at Haslar Hospital, Portsmouth, recalls that on the day she was to go overseas she had a letter from Wakefield's to say her navy shirts were in. She phoned to say it was too late to pick them up. When she arrived at Waterloo station Desmond Wakefield was waiting at the barrier with her shirts, having come up all the way from Horsham especially to give them to her.

Crashed German aircraft were exhibited in the town to boost morale and raise funds to buy a Spitfire for Horsham to donate to the forces. £5,000 was raised, Stan Parsons working tirelessly to achieve this goal, and on 9 January 1942 the *WSCT* printed a picture of the plane, Spitfire W3327. Unfortunately the plane had been shot down whilst on an air-sea rescue escort mission on 21 October 1941 and the Pilot Officer lost at sea. Children were encouraged to participate in the war effort and rose to the challenge in a variety of ways. At the High School for Girls pupils knitted jumpers for refugee children, collected money for refugee projects and wrote to French 'pen-friends'. Like many other women, the staff knitted fishermen's jerseys, socks, hats and scarves. Boys at Victoria Road Council School sold bars of 'Toilet and Victory Soap'. At other schools children collected rosehips to make vitamin-rich syrup for babies, acorns for pig food and horse chestnuts for the chemical industry.

Some residents billeted airmen who worked at the two aerodromes in the area at Gatwick and Faygate. The men were picked up in the mornings in long trailers and returned home again at night. Others billeted evacuees from London. Evacuees from Mercers School in London came to Collyer's School. Life was supposed to carry on as normal in the schools, but it was difficult with the fluctuating numbers of evacuees. At the High School for Girls external examinations continued as normal, but during air raids the girls were forced to continue writing their papers by candlelight in the brick shelters erected in the school grounds. During the summer holiday of 1940 the staff stayed on and became land girls lifting mangolds and potatoes.

The town escaped with relatively little destruction to buildings and infrastructure compared with other places, and was fortunate to escape major bomb damage during the Battle of Britain in 1940. The impacts of the dogfights overhead remain etched on people's memories. Mrs Pauleen Crowder, *née* Styles, as a child of three living at Rudgwick, retains as one of her earliest recollections the memory of her cousin John Morris, who is my father, lying flat on his back on the lawn staring up at the action in the sky in sheer amazement and totally oblivious to personal danger. The events surrounding D-Day, when the vivid description of a 'carpet' in the sky was applied to aircraft flying overhead, remains another abiding memory for many residents.

Several planes fell in the forest around Horsham and people went eagerly in search of souvenirs. Parachutes were highly prized as the silk could be used to make clothing. Swastika panels from the planes were much sought-after trophies. Nineteen German aircrew were buried in Hills cemetery; in the 1950s they were reburied in the German War Cemetery at Cannock Chase, Staffordshire which contains the bodies of all German servicemen who died

144 *'Monty' greets Sussex cricketers before the match between Sussex and Glamorgan on 1 June 1946. Left to right: P.A. Carey, C. Oakes, G. Cox, J. Nye, J. Oakes, J. Cornford, J. Langridge.*

in the United Kingdom during both world wars. On 31 March 1941 Sergeant Pilot Ernest Bloor died when his Hurricane of No. 1 Squadron Tangmere crashed into a cornfield in Pondtail Road, his parachute unopened. Bloor Close is named in his memory.

Nearly two hundred service personnel and local civilians associated with Horsham died during the war. In the town itself seven people were killed when Orchard Street was bombed in November 1940. Incendiary and high-explosive bombs landing in the town and surrounding countryside caused localised damage to buildings, and some residents were injured. The Gocher family, who lived at Amies Mill Cottage in Kerves Lane, had a lucky escape when two American-built Mitchell bombers crashed nearby on the night of 8-9 June 1943. An engine tore through the roof and ended up in the baby's cot. Fortunately the cottage was empty at the time. In the same year the Wimblehurst-Richmond Road area and the Guildford Road were bombed. The railway line was hit near the Worthing Bridge in November 1940; a goods train destined for Portsmouth

carrying 16 wagons crashed into the crater but no one was injured. In December 1943 the High School for Girls was machine-gunned and sustained minor damage, and the incident was reported in the *Daily Telegraph*.

Twice as many Collyerians died as in the First World War. Many of them having joined the RAF died in aerial battles, or from wounds sustained in their planes. The most highly decorated Old Collyerian was Major John Sehmer, MBE, killed in Mauthausen concentration camp after having been captured whilst trying to organise an uprising against the Germans in Slovakia. The SS man who caught him was arrested for war crimes in January 2004 aged 86, having participated in the killing of about one hundred and sixty people, mostly women and children. In February 2004 a group of students from Collyer's School laid a wreath for Sehmer in the gas chamber where he was executed.

The stationing of thousands of troops from Canada and America, and from the Free Armies of Europe, occurred on sites around Horsham. Roffey had an army camp on the old First

World War site, now Church Road, Birches Road, Furzefield Road and Bracken Grove. Denne Park was requisitioned by the military authorities, like other large houses and estates in the surrounding area, and used as a camp for French Canadian troops. The troops were amazed to find their Nissen huts placed in a deer park; one Canadian recalls that the deer were rapidly converted into steaks and chops. The town became the headquarters of a tank brigade, and the only significant traffic was made up of army convoys of huge lorries and tanks.

On Saturday or Sunday afternoons the main road was lined with soldiers heading for the movie, theatres, pubs or the Young Men's Christian Association, all popular places of entertainment. The 'soldiers in blue' contributed towards the social life of the town when, according to Dr John Dew, 'the town was suddenly flooded with Sweet Caporal cigarettes, and the hastily arranged dances were filled to capacity'. Many of these were held at the Drill Hall, which featured the largest sprung wooden floor in Sussex, and were extremely popular. There is no doubt that the Canadians boosted the morale of the town, and many local girls went back as brides to Canada. The men appreciated the

145 *The newsagent at 60 North Street, close to the railway station, was owned by Arthur Sheppard but has now been demolished. It was popular with commuters and those using the trains. This horse, owned by HUDC, was a regular visitor who came right up into the entrance of the shop to receive his daily sweets ration.*

146 *Gas works before demolition. The gasometers were familiar landmarks. An aerial photograph of 1932 reveals that the largest had 'HORSHAM' written across it. After demolition the site was turned into a car park. The building of a new YMCA Y centre for 48 young people started in 2004.*

hospitality of many of the residents, and friend-ships were formed which have stood the test of time. The old infirmary in Crawley Road was turned into a base hospital, the Canadian No. 1 General Hospital. Many wounded and disabled Canadians were placed there when they returned from the disastrous Dieppe Raid on 19 August 1942 and after D-Day on 6 June 1944. During the build up to D-Day Horsham was flooded with military personnel as various army units were stationed there.

A contingent of Polish troops was stationed at Farlington School, and for a long time the Poles held a monthly Polish Service in the Memorial Chapel in the parish church. After the war many refugees settled at Strood Green and integrated into the local community, finding domestic jobs in local establishments and some becoming naturalised.

In St Leonard's Forest near St John's Church, Hammerpond Road was a huge prisoner-of-war camp for Eastern Europeans. The prisoners would stand behind the high wire fences waiting for passers-by; cigarettes and tobacco from the locals would then be exchanged for hand-carved wooden toys. Italian prisoners of war worked on the farms. They were cheerful and friendly, glad to be out of the war. They wore brown uniforms with large yellow patches to identify them as prisoners of war.

A prisoner of a completely different kind, the acid-bath murderer, was held in Horsham in the aftermath of the war. In 1949 John George Haigh was brought to the Magistrates Courts at the Town Hall accused of the murder of Mrs Olive Durand-Deacon at Crawley. The sensational nature of the crime aroused enormous local and national interest. Within Horsham a few people were directly associated with the proceedings: Haigh was represented by John Ireland Eager, senior partner of Eager and Sons, 2 North Street, Horsham, who was a hard-working and leading figure in the town, known as 'Jack' to his colleagues and 'Mr Ireland' to his staff; Sir Hartley Shawcross stood for the prosecution as the Attorney General; Haigh sold the jewellery he had stolen from Mrs Durand-Deacon to Walter Bull, who owned a jeweller's shop in Middle Street. The murder headquarters for what turned out to be one of the 20th century's most famous cases was the police station in Barttelot Road, where Haigh was held in Cell No 2. Tried at Lewes Crown Court, he was finally found guilty of killing six people and disposing of their bodies in drums of sulphuric acid. He was executed.

An interesting insight into another, less gruesome, aspect of post-war life in Horsham is provided by the memories of the late Miss O. Linnell, District Nurse, which she recorded a few years ago for Dr Dew. She was reminiscing about the time when she lived at the Queen's District Nurses' Home, 52 Hurst Road before the district nurses relocated to new flats in Oakhill Road. The National Health Service came into being in 1948 and healthcare became

free at all points of access. Nurse Linnell would have met with a grateful public as a midwife because pregnant mothers no longer felt they must manage without medical services if they could not afford the doctors' fees. The Nurses' Home had a resident staff of six, who included district nurses, midwives and health visitors. All had a heavy workload as they covered Southwater, Barns Green, Horsham, Roffey and Broadbridge Heath. Miss Linnell wrote:

Twice yearly nurses from all Horsham Districts came for fittings for new uniforms, from earlier Norman Hartnell [of Mayfair] and latterly from Egerton Burnetts Ltd, [the nurses' outfitters in Buckingham Palace Road.] All nurses were expected to wear hats, full uniform and protective clothing at all times … No one was permitted to read the daily newspapers or to attempt the crossword before Miss Maskell [the Senior Nurse]. When fairly new there, I did this unpardonable sin and was never allowed to forget it … we all went to Evensong at St Mary's Church on Sundays, unless out on a case. Never mind if the Midwife had been up all night – maybe would be on the coming night; what benefit one got from the service is difficult to say, with eyes and heads dropping and having to be prodded awake. We had a day off a week and usually escaped as soon as possible out of reach … Midwives visited Delivered Mothers twice daily for a week, all mothers kept in bed for that length of time … In early days transport was by bicycle, not easy particularly up Farthing's Hill, when the blue Midwifery case was held precariously on the back. Never having ridden a bicycle until coming to Horsham, many an ungainly tumble took place. Fathers-to-be often had to return to the Nurses' Home to collect the Gas and Air Machine, quite an awkward and heavy model.

The ever expanding post-war population created pressure on land. Large residential estates were built containing private or council homes. The Cootes Farm Estate to the north of Guilford Road was built around an existing pond in the 1950s and, further north, council homes were built on the Spencers Farm Estate. To the east council houses were built between Highlands and Brighton Road. The Needles Estate was laid out south-west of the town from around 1955. Certain areas were reserved for new schools and playing fields in the western, south-western and eastern parts of the town. More recently, Horsham District Council (hereafter HDC) has been instrumental in supporting the establishment of industry and businesses in selected areas, particularly on sites adjacent to the Nightingale Road, Foundry Lane, Parsonage Way, Redkiln Way and Blatchford Road.

The 1944 Education Act, making provision for secondary education up to the age of 14 (and later 16), meant that new schools had to be built. Two new secondary modern schools were created in the eastern part of Horsham: Millais School (named in memory of J.G. Millais) for girls in Depot Road, and Forest School for boys in Compton's Lane. A secondary Technical School for boys had been built in 1943 in Compton's Lane, responding to pressure from local builders to train boys for the building trade, but this closed in 1958. In the 1970s, with the arrival of comprehensive education, there were further changes. The Girls' High School became a mixed comprehensive and was renamed Tanbridge House School, Millais

147 *The Meter Room is on the left of the picture. During demolition of the gas works a tunnel from a cellar of the former Allen Brothers' Malthouse, which was nearby in Springfield Road, was discovered running underneath the road to what had once been fields on the opposite side. This may have been used for illicit purposes, as malt that had not had duty paid on it was stored there in the 1830s.*

turned into a girls' comprehensive and Forest a boys' comprehensive. Tanbridge House School was relocated to a new purpose-built site at Farthings Hill, off the Guildford Road, in the early 1990s, and the house was converted into flats, while Tanbridge Park was developed into a residential complex. The grounds of the old Manor House School, used initially as the Junior School of Millais and Tanbridge but latterly by Tanbridge only, were sold for the building of a new Sainsbury's superstore. Collyer's also saw changes as it was turned into a Sixth Form College in 1976 and then expanded on its site in Hurst Road. The college was renamed the College of Richard Collyer in 1992, following a further reorganisation of Further and Higher Education.

There have been changes in the primary schools in the town too. These include the creation of Greenway County Primary School, which opened in 1950 for junior children from the burnt down Victory Road school, and the opening in 1949 of Trafalgar County Infants, which replaced Victory Road Infants. A new St Mary's Primary School has been built on the site of the Denne Road Girls' school, which had replaced the second Collyer's School built in 1840. The foundation stone was dedicated by the Bishop of Chichester in 1965 and laid by the Queen Mother. St John's Catholic Primary School was built south-west of the town in Blackbridge Lane in 1967. The Queen Elizabeth II Silver Jubilee School, for children with severe learning difficulties, was built in 1977 on the site of an old farm (Highlands Farm) on the northern part of the Forest School site.

Commercial competition from the new town of Crawley, whose expansion was rapid, and the development of Gatwick Airport as an international airport meant that Horsham needed to transform itself if it was to retain businesses and trade and remain economically buoyant. The Highlands Farm Estate, built in

148 *J.G. Millais, the son of the pre-Raphaelite painter John Everett Millais, was a soldier, hunter, naturalist and travel writer who lived at Compton Brow, which was demolished in the 1960s. His sculpture,* Black Grouse, *is in the garden of the Horsham Museum created by Sylvia Standing as an 18th-century herb and rose garden.*

the 1970s, was designed with the businessman in mind and was advertised as such in the *Financial Times*. The provision of industrial estates encouraged firms to come to Horsham, and this led to an expansion of employment opportunities. The Royal Society for the Prevention of Cruelty to Animals moved its headquarters to the Manor House in the Causeway in the 1970s and the CIBA factory expanded in the 1960s and '70s, creating more work for local people. The company based off Wimblehurst Road, known now as Novartis Pharmaceuticals UK, together with the new research establishment – Novartis Horsham Research Centre – remains one of the main employers in the town.

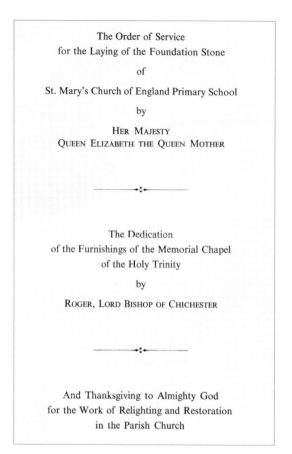

The Order of Service
for the Laying of the Foundation Stone

of

St. Mary's Church of England Primary School

by

HER MAJESTY
QUEEN ELIZABETH THE QUEEN MOTHER

---❖---

The Dedication
of the Furnishings of the Memorial Chapel
of the Holy Trinity

by

ROGER, LORD BISHOP OF CHICHESTER

---❖---

And Thanksgiving to Almighty God
for the Work of Relighting and Restoration
in the Parish Church

149 *This service took place on the Feast of the Annunciation of the Blessed Virgin Mary (25 March).*

The most significant development was the arrival of major insurance company Sun Alliance, which established headquarters in the town when it moved into Stocklund House in 1964. With over 800 employees Sun Alliance presented a wealth of career opportunities to residents in Horsham and the surrounding area and became the key employer. It gave the town a boost and arrested the threat of economic decline.

Traffic problems in the town centre were caused by increasing numbers of vehicles on the roads. Attempts to regulate the traffic were made in 1959 with the introduction of a one-way system known as 'Barker's Bite', after the Superintendent of Police at the time. Nairn and Pevsner referred disparagingly to Horsham in the early 1960s as 'an exasperating, traffic-laden, half-realised town. Traffic winds through it and parked cars flood pretty streets too small in scale to take them. Removal of through traffic would make it a very different place.' The HUDC was forced into taking more drastic action, and some rather uncoordinated development followed which included constructing a dual carriageway as an inner ring road, diverting traffic from West Street, and building the open-air shopping precinct of Swan Walk. The changes entailed the loss of some roads and old buildings, such as the burgage property of Bornes, the *Black Horse Hotel* and the medical practice at 15 North Street, which had to be demolished to make way for a new roundabout. The surgery, which had been opened in 1913 on land opposite the former St Mark's Church, had been one of the earliest purpose-built surgeries in the country, complete with dispensary. The second purpose-built surgery, this time in Albion Way, was opened in 1972 and was regarded as a showpiece, designed to accommodate the increasing demands of the NHS. The premises, in time, proved to be inadequate, and so the building was pulled down. The new Park Surgery has recently replaced it.

The huge post-war expansion of the town (which had a population of over 27,000 in 1970), economic changes and altered lifestyles required an overall modernisation programme if the town were to cope with the growing use of the car and keep its customers. The opportunity presented itself with the creation of the HDC in 1974 and the provision of professionally trained executives.

NINE

The Transformation of a Town

The last three decades of the 20th century have seen more changes in the history of Horsham than during the entire course of its history, changes deemed necessary if the town were to continue as a dynamic centre in the 21st century. The HDC was given the power and expertise to oversee changes, and an estimated £230 million has since been invested on behalf of the population of around 40,000 people (in 2000). This achievement was made possible by community and businesses working together. The principal investors have been Norwich Union, Royal & SunAlliance, J. Sainsbury Developments Ltd,

150 *Driving sheep along the roads on market day used to be a familiar sight. Today Hurst Road is a busy through-road with key buildings including Northbrook College of Further and Higher Education, Collyer's Sixth Form College, the Post Office Sorting Centre, Police, the Ambulance and Fire Stations, the Law Courts and the Community Hospital.*

Sainsbury's, Tesco's, Waitrose, Marks & Spencer and Allders, who have all had the confidence to sponsor developments.

The HDC involved the community in a two-year consultation exercise as it juggled the need to preserve and enhance the historic heart of the town yet provide a better road system, safe areas for pedestrians, improved shopping and expanded leisure facilities. Imaginative business opportunities and purchases of land enabled the transformations to go ahead. Whilst they were meant to benefit the local community, it was painful for many older residents, who knew and loved Horsham as it was in pre-war days, to watch such radical alterations.

The five overlapping phases of redevelopment included freeing the resources and space for extending the inner road system by relocating the Tesco's store to Broadbridge Heath,

the pedestrianisation of the Carfax, the Piries Place redevelopment and the new Sun Alliance complex, the pedestrianisation of the Bishopric and a new leisure centre at Broadbridge Heath. The Blackhorse Way site, which included the new Forum with its water features and sundial and an extended Sainsbury's, Allders, the surgery, the public library, the bus station, flats and a car park, finally completed the scene. Horsham has won national prizes, including two Civic Trust awards, for its town plan schemes, and the culmination of these years of change took place with the royal visit of the Queen and Prince Philip on 24 October 2003 to unveil the Horsham Heritage Sundial and open the refurbished Capitol Arts Centre.

The spacious Horsham Park, with its gardens and recreational and sporting activities, is used by members of the public of all ages. The

151 *Horsham's association with horses is depicted in this sundial, which was commissioned by the Horsham District Council for the Millennium.*

152   *The Hurst family created attractive gardens before they gave the park to the town. The 56 acres of parkland has since been developed and nurtured to provide a pleasant area for the public.*

provision of a bowling alley and night club at the former Park Recreation Centre, and the new swimming and leisure facilities known as the Pavilions, which contains the third pool to be built on this site, have proved to be welcome amenities. The new bandstand beside the pleasant Conservatory Café enhances the park, especially in the summer months when concerts are performed. A distinctive feature is the Millennium Maze with its sculpture of the St Leonard's Forest Dragon. The creation of the maze was a collaborative community project, which involved residents in sponsoring bricks and Millais School in planting the hedging.

Some changes have met with hostility and controversy. There has been criticism of certain architectural styles and the high density of building especially near the town. The decision by Sun Alliance to develop their premises caused much acrimony as this necessitated the pulling down of St Mark's Church. Only the spire was left and this now accommodates the Horsham Volunteer Bureau. The church was, however, beset with problems: it was in need of repair, was marooned by the traffic system and had a dwindling congregation. The Church Commissioners declared it redundant in April 1989 and complete clearance of the site then began for the development of St Mark's Court as headquarters for Sun Alliance. By way of compensation Sun Alliance agreed to finance a new St Mark's Church in the expanding part of the town in the North Heath Lane area. This is now one of the five churches in the parish of Horsham in a Team Ministry, the others being St Mary's, Holy Trinity, St Leonard's and St John's in Broadbridge Heath.

153 *A view of the parish church after restoration in the 19th century, with the heavily buttressed tower and the broach spire, which is a common feature in Sussex. This one is covered with 50,000 wooden shingles. The weather vane is a cockerel. During repair work in 1973 the beak and head, made of cast copper, were estimated to be 400 years old.*

Other difficult decisions included the demolition of the Capitol Theatre, although the conversion of the ABC Cinema in North Street into a new Arts Centre was intended to rectify this loss. The building of the new Sainsbury's supermarket at the heart of the town, reversing the trend for out-of-town retail development, has proved to be a successful move despite initial apprehension.

On 14 April 1992 demolition of Stocklund House began and was a welcome move. Prudential Assurance had built this 10-storey tower block with the approval of the old HUDC, but it towered over the town and was an unpopular development. The demise of the building removed an ugly blot from the town.

Sun Alliance amalgamated with the Royal Insurance Company to become Royal &

SunAlliance in 1997. Their new complex of harmonised, high quality and self-contained buildings has transformed that part of the town. Besides employing upwards of 2,000 people in the town and at Southwater, the company has also given significant amounts of financial assistance to local organisations, and its involvement with community activities has been highly valued by Horsham people. It works closely with the HDC supporting activities such as 'Horsham in Bloom', Arts Fanfare and Christmas Lights. The HDC and Royal & SunAlliance provided the garden at Park House for the disabled, blind and partially sited.

Horsham in Bloom has been singularly successful. In only a few years its impact on the town has been astounding and is a tribute to all those involved with the charity. It has won

154 *The Carfax, summer 2004. Floral decorations adorn the lamp-post bearing the Twinning Plaque. The roundels at the rear of the War Memorial can be seen in the background.*

155 *Mr Pirie was often seen driving a donkey and trap. He purchased land and built 15 cottages for the poor and the area became popularly known as Pirie's Alley. He was headmaster of Collyer's from 1822-67 and revived the school, which was in a reclining state. Under his initiative the old school buildings in Denne Road were replaced in 1840.*

156 *A sign of the times as individually owned shops succumb to competition from chain stores.*

an impressive number of awards, as a regional, national and international winner. This has been achieved through a 'Horsham in Bloom' committee supported by local businesses, organisations, residents and the HDC, many of whom have provided sponsorship. 'Horsham in Bloom' not only provides floral displays, but has improved and enhanced the town in other ways. Helped by Novartis, the care of the environment is given a high priority.

The Lynd Cross area, with the striking Shelley Fountain, the pedestrianised Carfax and the new Forum, provides pleasant public spaces for shoppers and residents. Spectacular sculptures are assets to the town centre: the 'Swans' in the Swan Walk Shopping Centre and 'Pirie's Donkey and Cart' in Pirie's Place are the work of Lorne McKean, the talented and nationally acclaimed sculptor. Her equally gifted husband, Edwin Russell, created the 'Celebration of Life Roundels' for the War Memorial. Their most recent contribution to Horsham, along with sculptor Damien Fennell, has been the 'Horsham Heritage Sundial' commissioned in the Millennium to celebrate the history of Horsham by the HDC. A three-dimensional, pierced bronze ring that portrays aspects of the rich heritage of the Horsham District, it is the focal point in the new Forum.

157 *This advertisement for Trelfer's appeared in the Rudgwick parish magazine in September 1948.*

**To Commemorate the Twinning of
HORSHAM
with
ST. MAIXENT L'ECOLE and LAGE
(FRANCE) (GERMANY)
The Original Plaque was Unveiled on 3rd May 1986**

Anthony Windrum, Chairman, Horsham District Council
Camille Lemberton, Mayor, St.Maixent, L'Ecole
Rudolf Niebuhr, Mayor, Lage

158 *Horsham was twinned with St Maixent L'Ecole in France in 1982, and with Lage in Germany in 1985.*

The completion of the road system and provision of car parks, whilst lamented by many, has sought to contain traffic and parking problems. The construction of the northern bypass, linking the A24 and the A264, led to rapid housing development in the northern part of Horsham on land bought from the Hurst family. This necessitated the creation of a new parish of North Horsham, incorporating Roffey, Little Haven and North Heath. The town now expands over the entire former Common, and the loss of agricultural land to bricks, mortar and concrete is deplored by some.

The closure of long established, independently owned local businesses, industries and retail outlets has been a phenomenon not just of the last few decades but the 20th century, in Horsham and elsewhere. One key example is Lintotts Engineering Ltd. The foundry had operated continuously since the 1890s supplying ironwork for the local council until it was shut down in 1962. The business diversified into general engineering and one of its specialities was the repair and maintenance of steam traction engines and steam ploughs. Another line started before 1914 was the installation and servicing of electric lighting plants, water supplies and heating systems. A specialisation in precision engineering began after the Second World War. In 1947 F.H. Ayling Ltd acquired the company and it was incorporated into Ayling Industries Group, but continued to provide employment for many – in 1962 there were over 650 employees and, at its peak, the annual turnover was £4½ million. The company was noted for its high standard of apprenticeship training, and son tended to follow father into the workshops. Long service was also a feature, with many employees working there for over 40 years. The works were closed in 1980 as a result of the economic recession.

A few independent trades remain in the Carfax, but in West Street the only one left is Wakefield's the jewellers. The closure of Wakefield's café, in particular, was met with much regret. The business had earned a high reputation as outside caterers and it was sad to see the end. Wakefield's had provided the

159   *The purpose of the Twinning Association is to promote and foster friendship with Horsham's twinned areas. Here members of the Twinning Association enjoy the hospitality of their friends in Lage.*

catering for some notable events, including the 21st birthday celebrations of Lord Cowdray and visits to Arundel Castle by the Queen. In East Street Trelfer's jewellery shop is located on premises that have provided this service since at least 1895 and probably even earlier, since in the 1841 census Mary Muzzell was listed here as a watchmaker. Horsham shops continue to provide variety and choice, but are now in the hands of national chain stores.

The 20th century has been shattered twice by world wars but, in common with many other towns, Horsham has forged new links. In 1982 the town was twinned with St Maixent L'Ecole in France, and three years later with Lage in Germany. The purpose of the Twinning Association has been to promote and foster friendship with

Horsham's twins, both personally and through organisations. Many exchanges have taken place between schools, music groups, sports clubs, churches, choirs and adult education groups, and the movement continues to flourish. French and German clubs have been established in the town for many years.

The challenge of retaining the character of this historic market town whilst meeting present-day requirements presents local people with a fine balancing act. For many people the controlled pace of change in Horsham has been its attraction. The continuous expansion in and around the town bears witness to the fact that Horsham is regarded as an attractive location in which to live and many take pride in the transformation of recent years.

Bibliography

Documents, reference works, directories, magazines, newspaper cuttings and ephemera have been consulted at the ESRO, WSRO, Worthing and Chichester Libraries and Horsham Museum. Sources for Quaker records include original documents of the Horsham Monthly Meetings at the Surrey History Centre, microfilms of births, marriages and deaths at WSRO, and general local records and wills at the ESRO and WSRO. The Friends' House Library is an invaluable source of general Quaker information. Other sources are as follows:

BOOKS
Albery, W. (ed.), *Reminiscences of Horsham being Recollections of Henry Burstow* (1911)
Albery, W., *A Parliamentary History of Horsham* (1927)
Albery, W., *Millenium of Facts in the History of Horsham and Sussex* (1947)
Andrew, M., *Francis Frith's Around Horsham* (2000)
Armstrong, J.A., *A History of Sussex* (1974)
Arscott, D., *The Sussex Story* (1992)
Arscott, D., *Horsham Past & Present* (2002)
Beswick, M., *Brickmaking in Sussex* (1993)
Bosworth, G.F., *Sussex* (1909)
Bowen, E.J., *The Enclosure of Horsham Common*, WSRO MP 1590 (1977)
Brandon, P. and Short, B., *The South East from A.D.1000* (1990)
Briffett, D., *The Acid Bath Murders* (1988)
Burgess, P. and Saunders, A., *Battle over Sussex* (1990)
Burgess, P. and Saunders, A., *Blitz over Sussex 1941-2* (1994)
Caffyn, J., *Sussex Believers: Baptist Marriages in the 17th & 18th century* (1988)
Cockburn, J.S. (ed.), *Calendar of Assize Records. Sussex Indictments, Elizabeth I* (1975)
Cobbett, W., *Rural Rides* (1830)
Cleere, H. and Crossley, D., *The Iron Industry of the Weald* (1985)
Coomber, G.H.W., *Bygone Corn Mills in the Horsham Area* (1996)
Dicks, J.E., *Extracts from Sussex Records* (1968)
Dicks, J.E., *Transcripts of Extracts from 'The Book of Suffering' of Friends in Sussex during the 17th & 18th centuries* (1972)
Djabri, S.C. and Knight, J., *Horsham's Forgotten Son: Thomas Medwin* (1995)
Djabri, S.C., *The Horsham of Thomas Charles Medwin 1776-1829* (1995)
Djabri, S.C. (ed.), *A little news from Horsham* (2002)
Djabri, S.C. and Smith, P., *Horsham – the development of a market town* (2002)

Djabri, S.C. (ed.), *The Horsham Calendar of Crimes and Criminals* (2003)

Djabri, S.C. (ed.), *The Diaries of Sarah Hurst 1759-1762* (2003)

Dodds, W., *Still Smiling Through. World War II Memories collected from among the congregation & Friends of St Mary's Church, Horsham* (2001)

Drewett, P., *Archaeology in Sussex to A.D. 1500* (1978)

Drewett, P., Rudling, D. and Gardiner, M., *The South-East to A.D. 1000* (1988)

Dudley, H., *The History & Antiquities of Horsham* (1973)

Elwes, D.G.C. and Robinson, C.J., *Castles, Mansions and Manors of Western Sussex* (1876)

Fletcher, A., *Sussex 1600-1660, A County Community in Peace & War* (1975)

Fletcher, C. (ed.), *Causeway, Horsham's Historical Magazine 1-12* (1972)

Fox, G., *A Journal or Historical Account of the Life, Travels, Sufferings, Christian Experiences etc of George Fox* (1694)

Glover, G., *'15 North Street.' A History of the Practice 1913-1972.*

Glover, J., *Sussex Place Names* (1997)

Goldsworthy, M., *The Sussex Bedside Anthology* (1950)

Goring, J., *Burn Holy Fire* (2003)

Hare, C., *Historic Sussex* (1998)

Harris, R. (ed.), *Weald & Downland Open Air Museum* (n/d)

Hayes, M., *William Penn in West Sussex, A lecture* (1994)

Holmes, F., *Horsham Cottage Hospital* (1980)

Hood, T., *The poetical works of Thomas Hood* (1892)

Horsfield, T.W., *History of Sussex, vols.1 & 2* (1972 reprint)

Hudson, T.P., *A History of Horsham* (1988)

Hughes, A. and Windrum, A., *Bygone Horsham* (1982)

Hughes, A., *Seven Horsham Houses* (1979)

Hughes, A., *Horsham Houses* (1986)

Hughes, A., *Shops and Shopping* (1989)

Hughes, A., *Causeway Houses* (1995)

Hughes, A., *North Horsham* (1995)

Hughes, A., *Down at the old Bull & Bush* (1997)

Hughes, A., *Chesworth* (1998)

Hughes, A., *Hell for Leather* (1998)

Hughes, A., *The King's Head* (1998)

Hughes, A., *'Clothing oft maketh man'* (1999)

Hughes, A., *'No more Twist'* (1999)

Hughes, A., *Hammer and Chisel* (1999)

Hughes, A. and Knight, J., *Hill's lost stately home and garden* (1999)

Hughes, A., Knight, J. and Williams, M., *Horsham District Heritage Trail* (2000)

Hurst, D., *Horsham: Its History & Antiquities* (2nd edition, 1889)

Judson, M.C. (ed.), *Off the Wall: A Catalogue of Horsham Museum's Poster Collection* (1999)

Kensett, E., *History of the Free Christian Church, Horsham* (1921)

Knight, J., *Horsham, its History 947-1990* (1996)

Liddell Hart, B. H. (ed.), *The Letters of Private Wheeler* (1951)

Lucas, E.V., *Highways & Byways in Sussex* (1904)

Marsh, T.W., *Some Records of the Early Friends in Surrey and Sussex from the original minute books & other sources* (1886)

Mitchell, V. and Smith, K., *Branch Lines to Horsham* (1982)
Mitchell, V. and Smith, K., *Crawley to Littlehampton* (1986)
Nairn, I. and Pevsner, N., *Sussex* (1965)
Neale, K., *Victorian Horsham: The Diary of Henry Michell 1809-1874* (1975)
Northcott, A., *Popular Entertainment in Horsham 1880-1930* (1988)
Robinson, M., *Wedded in Prison & other Quaker Stories* (1925)
Russell, M., *Prehistoric Sussex* (2002)
Scarry, S.J., *Horsham's Hidden Horrors* (1996)
Seward, D., *Sussex* (1995)
Straker, E., *Wealden Iron* (1969)
Swinfen, W. and Arscott, D., *Hidden Sussex* (1984)
Thistlewaite, B., *Bax Family, An Account of the Early Quakers* (1936)
Tyler, E.J., *The Clockmakers of Sussex* (n/d)
Victoria County History, *A History of Sussex* (1905)
Wales, T., *An Album of Old Horsham* (1989)
Wales, T., *Fabulous Horsham* (1990)
Wales, T., *Horsham & District in Old Photographs* (1994)
Wales, T., *Horsham Then and Now* (2000)
Wallace J. (comp.), *Images of Sport: Sussex County Cricket Club* (2001)
WSRO, *D-Day West Sussex* (1994)
White, C., *Horsham Town & Country 'When the Siren Sounded'* (1995)
Wield, E.M., *Elizabeth Gatford 1741-99* (1999)
Willson, A.N., *A History of Collyer's School 1532-1964* (1965)
Winbolt, S.E., *History of the Parish Church of St Mary the Virgin Horsham* (1941)
Windrum, A., *Horsham, An Historical Survey* (1978)
Woolley, M., *The Quakers in Chichester 1655-1967* (1998)

HORSHAM SOURCES
An Illustrated Guide to Horsham Parish Church of St Mary the Virgin
Horsham District Council & West Sussex County Council, *Horsham mapped. A catalogue of Local
   Maps* (1998)
Horsham Heritages, vols 1-10
Horsham Museum, *Memories from a Town that disappeared: Horsham during World War II* (1989)
Horsham Museum, *Horsham Ringers Peal Book* (1991)
Horsham Museum, *The Story of the Patriot Engineers 1942-5* (1991)
Horsham Museum Society & Horsham Photographic Society, *Then & Now Horsham* (2001)
The Horsham Society, *The Horsham Town Trail for Children* (n/d)

ARTICLES
Attree, F.W.T. (ed.), 'Post Mortem Inquisitions 1485-1649', *Sussex Record Society*, vol.14 (1912),
   p.227
Beckensall, S.G., 'The Excavation of Money Mound', *Sussex Archaeological Collections*, vol.105
   (1967)
Blunt, W.S., 'Extracts from Mr J. Baker's Horsham Diary', *Sussex Archaeological Collections*, vol.52
   (1909)
Caffyn, J., 'Sussex Schools in the eighteenth century', *Sussex Record Society*, vol.81 (1998)
Chapman, J., 'The Enclosure of Horsham Common', *Sussex Archaeological Collections*, vol.120 (1982)

Cooper, J.H., 'A Religious Census of Sussex 1676', *Sussex Archaeological Collections*, vol.45 (1901), p.146

Cooper, J.H., 'Return of Conventicles in Sussex in 1669 & King Charles' Licences for Nonconformists in 1672', *Sussex Archaeological Collections*, vol.51 (1908)

Daniel-Tyssen, J.R., 'Parliamentary Surveys of the County of Sussex A.D. 1649-1653', *Sussex Archaeological Collections*, vol.23 (1871), p.280

Djabri, S., 'The Tredcrofts of Horsham – confusion among the records', *Sussex Family Historian*, vol.13, no.7 (September 1999)

Farrant, J., 'Sussex Depicted: Views & Descriptions 1600-1800', *Sussex Record Society*, vol.85 (2001)

Figg, W., 'Extracts from Documents illustrative of the Sufferings of the Quakers in Lewes', *Sussex Archaeological Collections*, vol.16 (1864)

Ford, W.K., 'Chichester Diocesan Surveys 1686 & 1724', *Sussex Record Society*, vol.78 (1994), pp.81-2

Garraway, R., *Sussex Notes & Queries*, vols 1 & 2 (1926 & 1928)

Garraway Rice, R. (ed.), 'Sussex Protestation Returns 1641-2', *Sussex Record Society*, vol.5 (1906), pp.97-102

Garraway Rice, R. (ed.), 'Sussex Apprentices & Masters 1710 –1752', *Sussex Record Society*, vol.28 (1924)

Garraway Rice, R.(ed.), 'Horsham Parish Register 1541-1635', *Sussex Record Society*, vol.21 (1915)

Godfrey, W.H. (ed.), 'Sussex Wills vol.II', *Sussex Record Society*, vol.42 (1936-7)

Godfrey, W.H. and Salzman, L.F., 'Sussex Views from the Burrell Collection 1776-91', *Sussex Record Society* (reissued 2001)

Grieves, K. (ed.), 'Sussex in the First World War', *Sussex Record Society*, vol.84 (2000)

Hudson, W. (ed.), 'The Three Earliest Subsidies for the County of Sussex in the years 1296, 1327, 1332', *Sussex Record Society*, vol.10 (1910)

Hunnisett, R.F., 'Sussex Coroners Inquests 1485-1558', *Sussex Record Society*, vol.74 (1985)

Johnstone, H., 'Churchwarden Presentments: Archdeaconry of Chichester', *Sussex Record Society*, vol.49 (1947-8)

Lucas, P., 'Some notes on the early Sussex Quaker Registers', *Sussex Archaeological Collections*, vol.55 (1912)

McCann, T. J., 'Sussex Cricket in the 18th century', *Sussex Record Society*, vol.88 (2004)

Ray, J.E. (ed.), 'Sussex Chantry Records', *Sussex Record Society*, vol.36 (1931)

Salzmann, L.F. (comp.), 'Sussex Fines: From 1 Edward II to 24 Henry VII', *Sussex Record Society*, vol.23 (1916)

Salzmann, L.F. (comp.), 'Sussex Fines: From 34 Henry III to 35 Edward I', *Sussex Record Society*, vol.7 (1907)

Swales, R.J.W., 'The Howard interest in Sussex elections', *Sussex Archaeological Collections*, vol.114 (1976), p.50

Tyssen, A.D., 'Sussex Church Bells', *Sussex Archaeological Collections*, vol.57 (1915)

Way, A., 'Notices of the Benedictine Priory of St Mary Magdalen, at Rusper', *Sussex Archaeological Collections*, vol.5 (1852)

Index

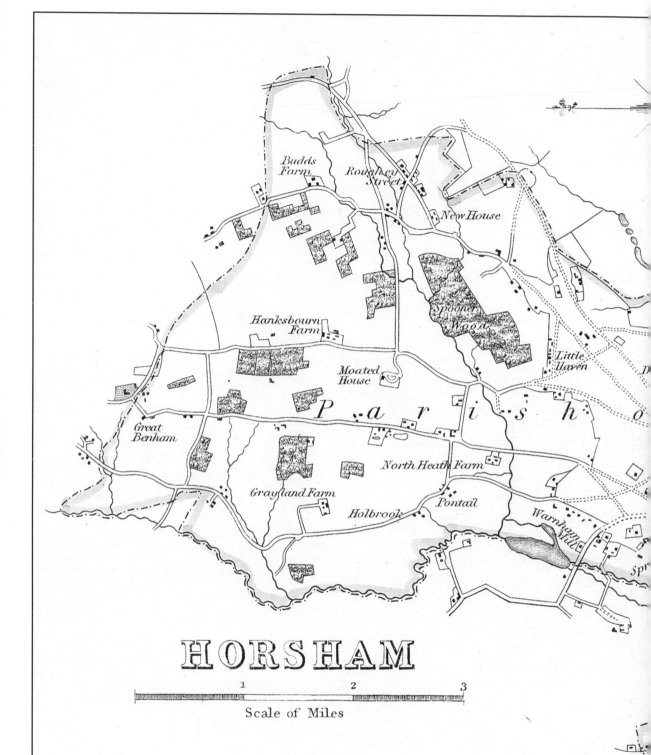

HORSHAM

1 2 3

Scale of Miles

Horsham drawn by Robert Creighton c.1835, engraved by J. & C. Walker for
Samuel Lewis' *Topographical Dictionary*. The map shows the parish of Horsham
and the borough boundary. Note north is to the left of the map.